THE
WHITE
ROSE

BY LILLIAN GROAG

DRAMATISTS
PLAY SERVICE
INC.

THE WHITE ROSE
Copyright © 1993, Lillian Groag

All Rights Reserved

SPECIAL NOTE

World Premiere at the Old Globe Theatre
San Diego, California.

For Barbara Iley Harris,
with love and gratitude.

THE WHITE ROSE was produced at the WPA Theatre (Kyle Renick, Artistic Director; Donna Lieberman, Managing Director) on October 15, 1991. It was directed by Christopher Ashley; the set design was by Edward T. Gianfrancesco; the costume design was by Michael Krass; the lighting design was by Debra Dumas; the sound design was by Aural Fixation and the production stage manager was Greta Minsky. The cast was as follows:

SCHMIDT	Roger Howarth
HANS SCHOLL	J.D. Cullum
SOPHIE SCHOLL	Melissa Leo
MAHLER	Victor Slezak
ROBERT MOHR	Larry Bryggman
BAUER	Brad Greenquist
ALEXANDER SCHMORELL	Michael Louden
CHRISTOPH PROBST	Roger Howarth
WILLI GRAF	Billy Morrissette

THE WHITE ROSE received its world premiere at the Old Globe Theatre (Jack O'Brien, Artistic Director; Thomas Hall, Managing Director) in February, 1991. It was directed by Craig Noel; the set design was by Ralph Funicello; the costume design was by Steven Rubin; the lighting design was by David F. Segal; the sound design was by Jeff Ladman and the stage manager was Douglas Pagliotti. The cast was as follows:

ROBERT MOHR	Jonathan McMurtry
ANTON MAHLER	J. Kenneth Campbell
HANS SCHOLL	John K. Linton
SOPHIE SCHOLL	Natalija Nogulich
BAUER	Tim Donoghue
ALEXANDER SCHMORELL	Steven Culp
CHRISTOPH PROBST	Bray Poor
WILHELM GRAF	Will Crawford
NURSE/MATRON	Sandra Lindberg
GUARDS	Jesus Ontiveros, Triney Sandoval

CHARACTERS

SOPHIE SCHOLL, 21
HANS SCHOLL, her brother, 25
ALEXANDER SCHMORELL, 25
CHRISTOPH PROBST, 24
WILHELM GRAF, 25
ROBERT MOHR, 50s, Head of the Munich Gestapo
ANTON MAHLER, 30s, Gestapo investigator
BAUER, Mohr's adjutant, 20s.

TIME and PLACE

Munich, 1942-43

NOTES ON STAGE AND
GROUND FLOOR DESIGN

This is a "chamber play." The setting should be extremely simple and non-realistic: levels, a minimum of furniture and only a hint of décor to indicate location. Sound, on the other hand, is important, and the author prefers that no substitutions be made for the music indicated.

FOREWORD

In 1942, a group of students of the University of Munich decided to actively protest the atrocities of the Nazi regime and to advocate that Germany lose the war as the only way to get rid of Hitler and his cohorts. They asked for resistance and sabotage of the war effort, among other things. They published their thoughts in five separate anonymous leaflets which they titled "The White Rose," and which were distributed throughout Germany and Austria during the Summer of 1942 and winter of 1943. They were apprehended and executed during February and April of 1943. All we know of the arresting officer is that, at the last moment, he tried to save their lives.

Today there are public monuments and memorials to their names throughout Germany and they are remembered yearly on the anniversary of their deaths by organizations of active and passive resistance the world over who meet at Perlacher Cemetery, just outside Munich, where they are buried. As the American Jewish Congress said on the occasion of the 1985 memorial: a Jew in Nazi Germany didn't have a choice. All these young people had to do to save their lives was to keep their mouths shut.

"There are some things which have not lived in vain."
e.e. cummings

The following is not biography, the domain of which I do not believe is the stage or screen, but an attempt to understand how certain catastrophes happen. We have all conveniently accustomed ourselves to consider "evil" as originating elsewhere: other people (preferably mentally imbalanced, but if pathology were not readily provable, then at least foreign), other places (never here, never with us, never next door), other governments (never our own). Most importantly, great national catastrophes are usually ascribed to amorphous masses of people, never taking into account that said masses are composed of individuals who, at one point or other, must have had a moment of choice. Above everything else, in our "glamorizing" of evil (by that I mean in our insistent placing it into the realm of the "exotic" and out of the common place) we have accustomed ourselves to view it as a premeditated leap of the mind into the unfathomable abysses of the soul; never as the gradual, imperceptible sliding into the moral chaos responsible for great communal disasters. In other words, the work of monsters, never of people like you or me.

THE WHITE ROSE

ACT ONE

A minimal multi-level set. Furniture and set-dressing are sparse. A table, light, a couple of chairs for Mohr's office, the same for the students' quarters. It's Munich, 1942-43.

While the house lights are still up the Haydn "Kaiser Quartet" begins to play. In the dark, the bells of a church — Munich's Frauenkirche — toll ten o'clock. Upstage, a caretaker is seen mopping the floor. Suddenly white sheets of paper float down to the ground all around him, like snow. He stops. Takes one up. Reads it. It registers. He looks up and shouts:

SCHMIDT.   Stop! Stop there! You, you, up there, stop!

DAY 1 — THURSDAY, FEBRUARY 18, 1943

Bells go off. Alarm sirens wail. A voice is heard over the loudspeakers.

V.O.   You are under arrest! Stay where you are! You are under arrest! Do not move. All doors are closed. Stay where you are. You are under arrest! *(There is an explosion of blinding white lights all directed C., where Hans and Sophie Scholl stand motionless, a small suitcase in hand. The sound of doors and gates clanking shut all around. Two men in dark overcoats come up to them.)*

MAHLER. Gestapo.

HANS. What —

MAHLER. Come with us please.

HANS. I'm in the armed forces —

SOPHIE. Why?

MAHLER. You can make your statements at headquarters.

SOPHIE. I want to call my parents —

MAHLER. You can do that at headquarters.

SOPHIE. We have classes to —

HANS. What's this all about?

MAHLER. Let's go. (*Blackout. Lights come up in an office at Gestapo Headquarters in the Wittelsbach Palace, in Munich. This office has a door the upper half of which is white, opaque glass through which we can see the silhouette of Bauer, Mohr's aide, in brown-shirt uniform. He's either seen in profile, motionless, or pacing, smoking, etc. He's never out of sight. Mohr is going through papers on his desk. He doesn't look up as he talks to Mahler who stands. There is an edge of irony in his voice that becomes apparent once in a while. An unreadable man. If Mahler notices, he doesn't react.*)

MOHR. They're here?

MAHLER. Yes, sir.

MOHR. How many?

MAHLER. Two, for the moment.

MOHR. Trouble?

MAHLER. I — don't — No, sir. (*Mohr looks up for the first time.*)

MOHR. I mean, did they resist arrest?

MAHLER. (*Beat.*) No.

MOHR. You're not certain?

MAHLER. (*Beat.*) They did not resist arrest, no.

MOHR. Witnesses?

MAHLER. The ... caretaker at the University.

MOHR. Evidence?

MAHLER. Just the leaflets ... at present.

MOHR. Circumstances?

MAHLER. They were seen dropping them from the first landing into the main hall.

MOHR. And...?

MAHLER. ... and they were arrested.

MOHR. By the janitor.

MAHLER. By the — a citizen's arrest, yes. This is what they were passing around: *(He reads from a paper, tonelessly.)* "Students! The German people look to us to break the National Socialist terror through the power of the spirit ..."

MOHR. The what?

MAHLER. The "power of the spirit." *(Beat.)* We have a check on their Aryan ancestry. *(Mohr pulls out some identification photographs from the pile of reports on his desk, and holds them up so Mahler can see them.)*

MOHR. *(Calmly.)* They look more Aryan than Frederic the Great.

MAHLER. Nevertheless —

MOHR. This wouldn't be another — *embarrassing* mistake, would it, Mahler?

MAHLER. Their father, a Robert Scholl has been arrested on at least one occasion for expressing himself in unflattering terms about the Führer.

MOHR. *(Beat.)* What did he say?

MAHLER. Something to do with ... livestock.

MOHR. Ah. Well, we're only investigating the individuals in question, Mahler. I am not interested in the prison records of their relatives.

MAHLER. Sir, I've been sent to Munich to —

MOHR. *(Good-humoredly.)* I've only had this job a week, do I already need "supervision?"

MAHLER. *(Laughing.)* Not at all, sir. I'm just here to assist.

MOHR. And to write reports. *(A moment of tension.)*

MAHLER. Sir?

MOHR. Berlin likes reports. Do you like reports, Mahler?

MAHLER. I —

MOHR. It's good to have an affinity for that sort of thing.

MAHLER. Reports?

MOHR. Paperwork. Mahler, I was promoted because I've been a good policeman for twenty-five years. I know my job.

MAHLER. That's a relief, sir. Bavarian Gestapo needs ...

MOHR. What?

MAHLER.   ... tightening up.

MOHR.   *(Beat.)* Why don't you bring me the girl first.

MAHLER.   *(Pause.)* She's — they're ... odd.

MOHR.   Odd?

MAHLER.   Schmidt said —

MOHR.   Schmidt?

MAHLER.   The janitor.

MOHR.   Ah.

MAHLER.   He said they did it quite openly. They were not trying to hide.

MOHR.   Then they've confessed.

MAHLER.   Not at all. They deny everything, and they're — they seem unusually — calm. *(Pause.)*

MOHR.   I want to take a look at them.

MAHLER.   I assure you, I've everything under —

MOHR.   I want to take a look at them. *(Mahler salutes and exits. The phone rings.)* Mohr speaking. Which newspaper? Put him through.... Yes, yes, Heil Hitler.... Yes, an arrest.... The Minister of Propaganda has not authorized a statement at the moment.... Pending investigation, yes.... We've no doubts as to the press's loyalty to the Reich, Herr Meyer, as you well know we release information on all treason cases.... Well, there hasn't been a hell of a lot going on lately — Certainly, we'll keep you posted. Heil — yes. *(He slams down the receiver. Bauer in brown-shirt uniform, an unthinking face and anodyne grin, escorts Sophie Scholl in. Mohr indicates a chair for her to sit on, and continues to look through the reports while he talks.)* Name?

SOPHIE.   Sophie Scholl.

MOHR.   Age?

SOPHIE.   Twenty-one.

MOHR.   Occupation?

SOPHIE.   Student at the University of Munich.

MOHR.   What do you study?

SOPHIE.   Biology and philosophy.

MOHR.   I thought girls went for literature courses.

SOPHIE.   Oh, I read a lot of ...

MOHR.   What?

SOPHIE.   ... things. Whatever is allowed — available.

MOHR. Love stories and such?

SOPHIE. *(Pause.)* Yes.

MOHR. Do you know what you're accused of?

SOPHIE. Something about some leaflets?

MOHR. You are suspected of co-authoring and distributing a set of pamphlets hostile in the extreme to the Führer, the Reich and the German War effort.

SOPHIE. Goodness.

MOHR. These pamphlets are, naturally, anonymous, and titled "The White Rose."

SOPHIE. I know nothing about it, sir. *(Pause.)*

MOHR. What were you doing in school? You've no classes today according to your schedule here.

SOPHIE. We decided to go home tonight. To Ulm. We had to let some friends know. *(Beat.)* Do you think we'll be able to catch the five o'clock train, sir? If not, I have to call home.

MOHR. You ... *suddenly* decided to go to Ulm? Why?

SOPHIE. Oh, mother ... you know how it is.

MOHR. And your entire luggage consists of an empty suitcase?

SOPHIE. What?

MOHR. When you were arrested, you were carrying an empty suitcase.

SOPHIE. Oh, for the laundry.

MOHR. The laundry.

SOPHIE. Mother does our laundry and we pick it up from her. *(Privately.)* Hans never washes his own clothes. Disgusting.

MOHR. Yes, well. Sophie ... is it?

SOPHIE. Yes, sir. *(Very clearly.)* Sophia Magdalene Scholl.

MOHR. Sophie, do you know the contents of the pamphlets in question?

SOPHIE. I've seen them around. Everybody has. So I have an idea.

MOHR. And you know what they say.

SOPHIE. ... I believe they call the Führer a ... charlatan, and a ... well, a mass murderer, and a —

MOHR. Ah ... yes, I —

SOPHIE. ... and a gangster, and —

MOHR. Yes, that's not what I —

SOPHIE. ... a sub-human, ... let's see, what else ...

MOHR. *(Quickly.)* There's no need to be specific —

SOPHIE. ... since you asked ...

MOHR. *(Overriding her.)* I am talking about the political implications of the ideas expressed.

SOPHIE. Politics? I don't know anything about politics.

MOHR. *(Looks at her for a moment.)* No ... *(Outside, the church bells toll the half hour.)*

SOPHIE. Church bells, next door! I love them!

MOHR. They give me a headache.

SOPHIE. *(Abruptly.)* He wanted to see Mathilde Schwarzkopf.

MOHR. Pardon?

SOPHIE. Hans. He wanted to see Mathilde Schwarzkopf.

MOHR. Mathilde Schwarzkopf?

SOPHIE. Our Youth Group Leader a few years ago.

MOHR. Hitler Youth?

SOPHIE. Of course! Both my brother and I were Group leaders. *(Confidentially.)* But she's no better than she should be, if you ask me. She went over to the boys' camp after hours.

MOHR. I see. Well, that's not really —

SOPHIE. *(Truculent.)* *Everybody* knows Mathilde Schwarzkopf in Ulm.

MOHR. I imagine they do. But —

SOPHIE. It's not as if she's pretty, or anything. She has an altogether alarming underbite. Of course, she's a blonde, and that's a plus —

MOHR. Yes, yes, but —

SOPHIE. *(On a roll.)* So there I am, stuck at home for the whole weekend, while Hans ... visits ... with old horse-face over there. I've better things to do with my life. Lots of homework. The Romantic poets this term, you know, and —

MOHR. Naturally. Could ... *(Mahler appears at the door.)* ... would you step out for a moment?

SOPHIE. Outside?

MOHR. Yes. Bauer! *(Bauer enters immediately.)* Escort Fraülein Scholl to the anteroom for a moment. *(Bauer and Sophie leave.)*

14

How are you doing with the boy?

MAHLER.   *(Wearily.)* He is uncommonly eager to talk ... about Aristotle, and glass painting, and theodicy. What the hell is theodicy?

MOHR.   Whatever it is, it's got to be better than the laundry and Mathilde Schwarzkopf.

MAHLER.   Beg pardon?

MOHR.   We do not seem to be on a ... fruitful path here, Mahler.

MAHLER.   Sir, we have a material witness and —

MOHR.   I'm afraid we're going to need a hell of a lot more than that. These are young Aryan individuals of some standing and ... visibility. The boy is in the *Army* — *(There is a knock on the door.)* Yes?! *(Bauer enters, a large dictionary in hand.)*

BAUER.   I looked up "theodicy" for Herr Mahler. It means *(Reading with difficulty.)* "vindication of divine providence in view of the existence of evil."

MOHR.   Ah, some other time, Bauer. *(Bauer salutes and exits.)*

MAHLER.   The janitor, the Schmidt individual saw them! He looked up when he saw the leaflets falling and he saw them!

MOHR.   He looked up into the light and he *thinks* he saw them. And there is a 3,000 mark reward that wouldn't do Herr Schmidt's pocket any harm.

MAHLER.   There's enough evidence —

MOHR.   North Africa, lost. Over 300,000 dead at Stalingrad. That boy has been on the Russian front. People are angry.

MAHLER.   It's precisely because of Stalingrad that Berlin wants those pamphlets stopped. The people's morale —

MOHR.   The people's morale won't be improved, I assure you, if we wrongfully arrest a war veteran, a *medic,* no less — look at these records — and a Girl Scout, on the word of a ... a Herr Schmidt!

MAHLER.   Girl Scout?

MOHR.   Both Scholls were leading members of the Hitler Youth. *(There is an awkward pause while Mohr pushes a pile of documents towards Mahler.)* You people are in too much of a hurry. You don't read *reports.* I want to send them home.

MAHLER.   Sir! Berlin —

MOHR.   This is Munich, Herr Mahler. *I* am in charge here.

MAHLER.   The circulation of the pamphlets has been ... extensive. They've reached Austria. Sir, as a representative of the Reich Minister of Justice, I must impress upon you: we need an arrest ...

MOHR.   *(Looking through dossier.)* But we've had arrests on this case, Mahler. Five in the last two months, to be precise. All *mistakes.* Last time it was two octogenarian spinsters from Hamburg who turned out to be related to General Rommel.... One of them claiming to be the Grand Duchess Anastasia.

MAHLER.   At this point, sir, even they would do.

MOHR.   Those are not methods I approve.

MAHLER.   New ideas require new methods, Herr Mohr. *(Mohr presses a buzzer on his desk.)*

MOHR.   I don't know anything about ideas, I am a police investigator. I don't like investigations to blow up in my face. *(Bauer enters.)* Bring me the Scholl boy. *(Bauer exits.)* I won't be needing you, Mahler. *(Mahler pauses and exits, crossing Bauer and Hans Scholl coming in. Mohr motions to the chair. Hans sits. Bauer exits and is visible just outside through the door-pane.)* Name?

HANS.   Hans Scholl.

MOHR.   Age?

HANS.   Twenty-five.

MOHR.   Occupation?

HANS.   Sergeant in the Second Student Medical Company. Munich University.

MOHR.   Do you know why you're here?

HANS.   Some misunderstanding about printing and politics.

MOHR.   Does the name "The White Rose" mean anything to you?

HANS.   Not really, no.

MOHR.   On the day of your arrest, that is today, Thursday, February 18, 1943, Jakob Schmidt, caretaker at the University states that he saw you and your sister Sophia scatter several hundred sheets of paper from the first landing of the central staircase into the main Hall. The content of these ... things is highly radical material and it's signed "The White Rose." Does that refresh your memory?

HANS.   There must be some mistake. Herr Schmidt is notoriously nearsighted.

MOHR.   *(Pause.)* You served as a medic in France and Russia?

HANS.   I am a medical student. I am a very bad shot.

MOHR.   Your father seems to have done the same in World War I.

HANS.   We're a ... traditional family.

MOHR.   You have a brother in the Eastern Front?

HANS.   Werner, yes. Good soldier. Decorated several times.

MOHR.   I see. And your father was mayor of several small towns.

HANS.   Yes. My father is ...

MOHR.   What?

HANS.   Very ... civically minded.

MOHR.   I've heard. *(Beat.)* The paper you tore up when you were arrested ...

HANS.   Somebody in the crowd pushed it in my hand, and I thought it might be incriminating, what with that Red Rose business and all —

MOHR.   White.

HANS.   Pardon?

MOHR.   It's "The White Rose."

HANS.   Oh. I thought it would be red. Being leftist propaganda.

MOHR.   It's not exactly "leftist."

HANS.   No?

MOHR.   There's a lot of twaddle about God in those leaflets.

HANS.   God! In this day and age?

MOHR.   But Mahler tells me you're somewhat interested in God.

HANS.   Interested?

MOHR.   You've taken a course in theodicy, or some such thing?

HANS.   Oh, that! It was part of a required course in philosophy.

MOHR. *(Pause.)* Do you believe in God?

HANS. *(Beat.)* It's rather ... an *excessive* idea, don't you think?

MOHR. *(Beat.)* That paper you tore up when you were arrested. We put it back together again. It contains defeatist ideas regarding the war and the Führer's military capabilities. It — proposes Franklin Delano Roosevelt as an ideal leader.

HANS. Well then, it *must* have been one of those Red Rose people, put it in my hand.

MOHR. *(Tired.)* White.

HANS. What?

MOHR. It's "White Rose."

HANS. Right.

MOHR. *(Beat.)* I understand that you were planning to go to Ulm today?

HANS. Yes, home for the the weekend. Pick up some clean clothes. My sister doesn't do her own laundry. Disgraceful.

MOHR. Yes, well —

HANS. *(Man to man.)* Actually, I'm seeing a girl there ...

MOHR. Would that be ... uh ... a Mathilde Schwarzkopf?

HANS. *(Very interested.)* You know Mathilde?

MOHR. No, I don't know Mathil — Fraülein Schwarzkopf!! Look, I'd like you to step outside for a moment. Bauer will get you some coffee, or what passes for it these days. Bauer! *(Bauer always just outside the door, enters. Mohr calls on the phone.)* Fraulein Schweder, get me Herr Mahler. *(To Bauer.)* See that Scholl here has coffee, or water, or whatever he needs.

BAUER. Coffee, sir?

MOHR. Yes, Bauer. You know, coffee. From beans. *(Bauer, astonished, salutes and exits with Hans. Mahler enters.)* Where is that report on the house search?

MAHLER. The search is still in progress, Herr Mohr. So far, nothing much —

MOHR. Nothing much. I'll give you all another fifteen minutes and I'm sending them home. This is a ridiculous waste of time. *(The telephone rings. Mohr picks it up.)* Hell – Heil Hit — Oh, hello, dear. Not much. No, actually, I've been discussing people's laundry and an unattractive young woman of apparently easy virtue called Mathilde Schwarzkopf. From Ulm....

Tonight? Let me see.... No, eight o'clock should be all right. At the Müllers'? That frightening child always bangs out the Moonlight Sonata after dinner. Certainly I like music — Oh, very well. Fine. Eight o'clock. Did you take Bismarck to the vet? Nonsense, he's never bitten anybody in his life! He just doesn't like red-headed people, that's all. By the way, I can't find my pocket watch ... the good one. Well, I did. I put it away for safety, and I can't remember where, that's all. Would you — Good.... Fine. Just tired. How's everything at home? Good.... Ah, yes, the garden gate. I'll fix it over the weekend. Yes, not safe.... No, nothing new. I'll talk to you later.... *(He hangs up the phone.)* Now, I've an important meeting at five, so —

MAHLER.   We've arrested several other students who might —

MOHR.   Careful! We don't want another student riot like last month's. Students get nervous when their classmates are arrested *erratically*. We can't afford nerves just at the moment.

MAHLER.   That wouldn't be repeated, sir. The Riot Police —

MOHR.   These kids are interested in being home for dinner, getting their laundry done — by their mother, I might add — and "visiting" a young woman with an unimpressive jaw-line. If not fundamentally dim, they're at best unimaginative. They didn't write those silly pamphlets.

MAHLER.   You consider those pamphlets harmless, sir?

MOHR.   Oh, for heaven's sake, listen to the tone of those things! The rantings of some religious fanatic, or a crackpot academic!

MAHLER.   They've been found everywhere. Schools, churches, factories, public transportation, theatres ...

MOHR.   Who's going to read them? People don't read. People go to the movies. Nobody reads! I'm sending them home. *(There is a knock on the door.)* Come in! *(Bauer enters with a report file.)*

BAUER.   It's from the investigators searching the Scholl quarters, sir. Here's their report. *(In handing it to Mahler, Bauer clumsily drops it. The papers scatter all over the floor. Bauer retrieves*

19

them and is extremely awkward doing it, so papers tear, fly under furniture, etc. Irritated, Mahler snatches them off his hands.)

MAHLER.   *(Reading.)* Well, well ...

MOHR.   Yes?

MAHLER.   They've found some stamps.

MOHR.   Stamps?

MAHLER.   Postage stamps, sir.

MOHR.   Let me understand this. We are about to accuse these innocuous young people of high treason, among other things, and our chief piece of solid evidence are some *postage stamps* found in their living quarters?

MAHLER.   Several *hundred* postage stamps. Of the same denomination used by the White Rose to mail their last leaflets. *(A silence.)* Shall we begin indictment proceedings? *(Lights up U.C. where Hans, Sophie, Willie Graf, Alexander Schmorell, and Christoph Probst stand. D., alone, Mohr picks up the pamphlets and starts reading them. In contrast to what we've seen of the students so far, they are passionate and aggressive. Their voices overlap and are punctuated by crowds shouting "Sieg Heil!" and by the sound of marching boots. Far in the distance the muffled voice of Hitler is heard, continuously ranting. Under that, Chopin's* Grande Polonaise in E Flat Major *is heard, first softly, then gaining in volume until it mingles with the kids' voices and eventually dominates the scene.)*

HANS.   "Nothing is so uncivilized for a nation as allowing itself to be ruled by an irresponsible gang that operates on base instinct." The White Rose, Munich, Summer, 1942.

SOPHIE.   "Freedom and honor ... this bloodbath has opened the eyes of even the stupidest German — The name of Germany is dishonored for all time if German youth does not finally rise ..." The White Rose, Munich, Summer, 1942.

SCHMORELL.   "... we yearn for the light in the midst of blackest night ..."   White Rose, 1942.

WILLI.   "Every word from Hitler's mouth is a lie." White Rose, 1942.

PROBST.   "The day of reckoning has come — the reckoning of German youth with the most abominable tyranny our people have ever endured."

HANS. "In the name of German Youth ..."

SOPHIE. "... we demand restitution by Adolf Hitler's state of our personal freedom ..."

SCHMORELL. "... the most precious treasure that we have ..."

WILLI. "... of which he has robbed us ..."

PROBST. "... in the most brutal way." The White Rose. Munich, 1942.

HANS. "It is a *moral duty* to put an end to this system."

SOPHIE. "We will not be silent. We are your bad conscience. The White Rose will not leave you in peace!" *(Mohr looks up. Blackout. The Chopin* Polonaise *stops and contemporary swing music of the 40s plays on the phonograph. It's a year ago. May 1942. Hans's rooms in the student boarding house. Sophie is dancing with Willi Graf and singing along. Christoph Probst attends to the phonograph, and Hans is trying to open a bottle of wine.)*

HANS. Turn it down, Sophie, the landlady! Decadent, enemy music!

SOPHIE. She only comes up when Willi plays his violin. She thinks we're tormenting her cat!

WILLI. Nobody here appreciates good music.

PROBST. We do! We're selling your fiddle!

WILLI. Laugh, laugh. They laughed at Paganini too. *(Probst pulls out photos from his pockets.)*

PROBST. Anybody for baby pictures? *(They all groan, but crowd around him, Hans still struggling with the corkscrew and the bottle of wine. They pass the pictures around.)*

SOPHIE. They've grown so much, Chris! They're beautiful!

HANS. Fine head of hair on that kid!

PROBST. That's the dog. This is the kid. And here's the other one. Perfect? *(Pointing at one of them.)* New tooth.

ALL. *(Ad-lib.)* Perfect! They look like you. Nah, too pretty. They look like their mother! The dog looks like you!

WILLI. What kind of dog is it?

PROBST. Don't know. We found him.

WILLI. This dog must be put under investigation!

ALL. *(Ad-lib.)* Check the dog! Check the dog! And its parents! Grandparents! Great-grandparents! Religion! Blood line!

Papers, papers, papers! Sexual habits! Bathroom habits! Eating habits! Any habits! *(They all pass around the picture of the dog. Willi ends up with the picture and climbs on a chair, sending up a lecture on "racial purity.")*

WILLI. *(Announcing.)* This dog is not Aryan!

SOPHIE. How can you tell, sir?

WILLI. Because he's not blond —

HANS. Like Hitler!

WILLI. Or tall —

SOPHIE. Like Goebbels!

WILLI. Or slender —

PROBST. Like Goering!

WILLI. This dog is ... of mixed blood! And ... *(He takes another look at the dog's picture. Thundering.)* IT'S BEEN FIXED! *(They boo and thumbs down the dog, etc. etc.)*

ALL. *(Ad-lib.)* A eunuch! A eunuch! Take it away! Take the owner too! *(Hans finally pops the cork out of the bottle. He and Sophie pour out the wine. Hans raises his glass in a toast.)*

HANS. The Allies! *(There's a knock on the door. Everybody freezes. Sophie takes the needle off the record. Another knock.)*

SCHMORELL. *(Off stage.)* Open the door, boys and girl! *(They relax.)*

WILLI. Wait, wait. Is this, to quote Dr. Goebbels, an "honest, intelligent, National Socialist?"

HANS. Can't be!

ALL. *(Going through the routine.)* And why not?

HANS. Because if he's intelligent and a Nazi he's not honest; if he's honest and a Nazi he's not intelligent. And if he's intelligent and honest ...

ALL. HE'S NOT A NAZI!

PROBST. Not so loud.

SCHMORELL. *(Off stage.)* Open the goddamn door! *(Sophie goes to the door. Schmorell enters carrying an old, beat-up mimeograph machine. He sets it down in the middle of the room. Probst quickly checks the hallway outside.)* Christ! You can be heard halfway down the hall.

PROBST. What's that?

SCHMORELL. One of the most beautiful things ever invented.

WILLI. Fine. But what is it?

HANS. *(Quietly.)* A printer. A duplicating machine. *(There is a silence. The "temper" of the room changes. Someone coughs nervously.)*

PROBST. Where'd you get it?

SCHMORELL. I stole it. *(They laugh feebly.)*

WILLI. What do you want it for?

SCHMORELL. I thought I'd use it in place of my bicycle. To print things of course!

WILLI. *(Uncomfortable.)* What things?

HANS. *(Quickly.)* Alex do you want some wine?

SOPHIE. I'll get another glass.

HANS. We're out. Get one from Franzel downstairs. *(She exits.)*

PROBST. Why, Hans?

HANS. "Unfit to vanquish — shall I meanly fly,
The one of all my band that would not die?"

PROBST. This is hardly the time for Byron.

HANS. Oh, I don't know. It may be *just* the time.

PROBST. We know what we think, isn't that enough?

HANS. No.

PROBST. Convictions don't change just because you can't flaunt them.

HANS. But they do. Little by little. *Nothing* is time-proof. Especially convictions.

WILLI. It's a dangerous choice.

HANS. Goes with life. *(Laughing.)* Even Adam and Eve had to choose, in order to become human.

PROBST. To become *mortal.* They were human before. They weren't counting on mortality.

WILLI. Oh, for heaven's sake. Are we going to sit around arguing about how many angels go through the eye of a needle —

SCHMORELL. Camels, Willi, camels.

WILLI. What?

SCHMORELL. It's camels for the needles and angels for the pins.

WILLI.   I think we've had too many philosophy courses. *(Raises his glass.)* To choice and mortality. Prosit! *(Another knock on the door. They all freeze again.)*
V.O.   Scholl! Telephone, female! *(Hans exits followed by wolf-whistles and cat-calls.)*
WILLI.   Women never call me, why is that?
SCHMORELL.   You're just too passionate a man, Willi. They're frightened.
WILLI.   *(Outraged.)* What — I have *never* — ! *(Sophie re-enters with a glass.)*
PROBST.   That's not what we hear from Mathilde Schwarzkopf.
WILLI.   What?! Never in a million years — !
SCHMORELL.   Or her sister Ermengard, for that matter!
WILLI.   ERMENGARD!! She looks like Stalin!
SOPHIE.   Never mind them, Willi. They're jealous because *you* are a gentleman, and they're pigs. Here you are, Alex.
SCHMORELL.   Oink, oink. *(Hans returns.)* "O flesh, flesh, how art thou fishified." I've a toast.
WILLI.   Let's hear it for God's sake!
SCHMORELL.   Lady, gentlemen — and swine — I give you: William Shakespeare!
ALL BOYS.   *(Ad lib.)* Goethe! Dante! Schiller! Lope! Shelley! Bertold Brecht! Calderón! Heine! Thomas Mann! *(They get stuck.)*
SCHMORELL.   Frank Sinatra! *(Laughter, and over it.)*
SOPHIE.   The printed word! *(Hans leans down to touch the mimeograph while they drink and the lights fade to black, then come up in Mohr's office. Mohr and Mahler in continued action.)*
MOHR.   What else?
MAHLER.   About that paper that Scholl tried to destroy when he was arrested: the handwriting matches perfectly that of a couple of letters we found in his room. From a Christoph Probst, in Innsbruck.
MOHR.   Contents?
MAHLER.   Unremarkable. But the handwriting is the same. *(Beat.)* He is also a member of the armed forces. Luftwaffe. Student Company. A medic. *(Pause.)*

MOHR.   Get in contact with his superior officers at once.

MAHLER.   There's no need to —

MOHR.   Surely you realize this is a ... an *awkward* time to be arresting members of the Armed Forces, Mahler. Without proper procedure.

MAHLER.   *(Beat.)* Now the girl —

MOHR.   Please. A mousy 20-year-old, not too terribly bright, as far as I can see, who would parrot anything her brother says. We'll put her to work in a munitions factory.

MAHLER.   It's not that simple, Herr Mohr.

MOHR.   I'm making it that simple Herr Mahler. I am a very busy man. *(Mahler exits. Mohr opens his desk drawer, takes out a bottle of aspirins, and takes two with a glass of water. He looks out the window. Stress begins to show. The bells from the Frauenkirche are heard. Cross lights with Hans's room. Sophie is sitting ram-rod straight on an armchair clutching an open book to her chest. Somebody outside approaches whistling the* Wiener Blut Waltz. *The door opens and Hans and Schmorell enter. It's very late at night.)*

HANS.   Sophie! What are you doing up?

SOPHIE.   Waiting.

HANS.   Oh, good. Are you hungry? We brought —

SOPHIE.   No.

SCHMORELL.   What's the matter? No letter from Fritz?

SOPHIE.   I don't write to Fritz anymore.

SCHMORELL.   *(Beat.)* I'm glad.

SOPHIE.   Someone has been passing around a leaflet. It's very interesting. Whoever they are, they call themselves "The White Rose." Imagine, my favorite flower!

HANS.   Really?

SCHMORELL.   It sounds like a perfume advertisement. *(Without taking her eyes off them, she pulls a crumpled piece of paper from her cardigan pocket. She reads.)*

SOPHIE.   "The Spartan code of law was based on the dangerous principle that human beings are to be considered means and not ends — thereby destroying the foundations of morality and natural law."

HANS.   *(Uncomfortable.)* That's Schiller, isn't it?

SOPHIE.   *(Picking up the book from the chair.)* I found the passage underlined in your book. *(Pause.)*

HANS.   I couldn't — go on just *talking* ... about it. Making jokes because we feel helpless. I don't like to feel helpless. I want to take them on!

SOPHIE.   You mean ... we go at them? Just like that?

HANS.   Not you. Just us.

SOPHIE.   Why not me?

HANS.   It's dangerous!

SOPHIE.   For you too.

SCHMORELL.   We're men.

SOPHIE.   Don't worry I'll carry smelling salts.

HANS.   I don't want you in this.

SOPHIE.   Too late.

HANS.   Stay out of it, Sophie!

SOPHIE.   I can't!

HANS.   You mean you won't!

SOPHIE.   Can't! I can't just ... knuckle under.

SCHMORELL.   Hubris.

SOPHIE.   Nobody asked *you!*

SCHMORELL.   Fine.

SOPHIE.   So stay out of this.

SCHMORELL.   Right.

HANS.   Aren't you afraid, Sophie?

SOPHIE.   I'm terrified. But the worst of it is, I'm so afraid, I think if I don't *do* something right now.... I'll start going along with them.

SCHMORELL.   Nonsense.

SOPHIE.   It isn't. We're no better than anybody else. Fear is the great mind killer.

HANS.   We could be found out any moment and —

SOPHIE.   They won't catch us! We're smarter, quicker — we're younger! And we're *right!* They can't catch us!

HANS.   I won't let you —

SOPHIE.   You used to take me everywhere with you.

HANS.   *(Peevish.)* Don't remind me. "Me too, me too!"

SOPHIE.   Hänsel ...

HANS.   Don't call me Hänsel in front of people!

SOPHIE.   Alex is not *people*.

SCHMORELL. Oh, fine.

HANS. What do we tell mom and dad? I'm supposed to be looking after you.

SOPHIE. Tell them we love them.

HANS. Don't get flippant with me Sophie!

SOPHIE. Then don't tell me what to do!

SCHMORELL. Hey, hey!

SOPHIE. Anybody talking to you?

SCHMORELL. No, no.

SOPHIE. *(To Hans.)* Do the others know?

HANS. No. And they never will. *(The door bursts open. Willi and Probst storm in, in a panic, waving the pamphlets around.)*

PROBST. What the hell do you think you're doing?

WILLI. *(Overlapping.)* Are you out of your minds?! *(Cross lights with Mohr's office.)*

MAHLER. We have Christoph Probst, sir.

MOHR. What else?

MAHLER. We've —

MOHR. What time is it? I don't have a watch.

MAHLER. Past midnight. *(Beat.)* We've also picked up a Wilhelm Graf. Belongs to all sorts of Catholic Groups.

MOHR. Yes, well. Religious types are not dangerous.

MAHLER. There's Bishop von Galen, sir. We can't arrest him and we can't shut him up. For the moment.

MOHR. *(Beat.)* You have great faith in the system, don't you, Mahler?

MAHLER. Lack of faith is unpatriotic sir. And unsafe. *(Mohr laughs.)* Sir?

MOHR. I always thought faith and safety mutually exclusive. Never mind. What about the other arrests?

MAHLER. More of the same. Nobody knows anything. Everybody likes the Scholls. Such a good family. So ... German. They couldn't possibly, etc. etc. One girl keeps referring us to a Professor Huber who apparently would be glad to attest to their good character.

MOHR. The "theodicy" professor?

MAHLER. He's very popular with a certain element. We're going to bring him in.

MOHR.   What else do we have on Probst?

MAHLER.   Twenty-four years old. Medical student, no previous arrests, married, three children.

MOHR.   Three! At least Frau Probst knows her duty to the Fatherland. *(Abruptly.)* Do you have children, Mahler?

MAHLER.   *(Beat.)* No.

MOHR.   Ah. I do. *(Awkward pause. Mahler waits, papers in hand, to continue "business.")*

MAHLER.   *(Carefully.)* The Graf boy. He's also a medic in the Second Student Company at the University. Now the girl —

MOHR.   *(Sharply.)* Leave the girl to me!

MAHLER.   Certainly, sir. I just wondered —

MOHR.   There's nothing to wonder about, Mahler. Whatever her brother may have done, I'm certain she's telling the truth. She knows nothing. Quite an ordinary girl.

MAHLER.   She seems ordinary to you sir?

MOHR.   Charlotte Corday doesn't exactly come to mind.

MAHLER.   No, nothing like that. But she's so ... calm. Does that seem ordinary to you?

MOHR.   That could be because she has nothing to worry about.

MAHLER.   Could be. Will there be anything else, sir?

MOHR.   Yes. Interesting as those postage stamps may be, I'm afraid they won't quite do the job.

MAHLER.   I don't understand.

MOHR.   Handwriting analysis, stamps ... if you'll forgive me, it sounds like something out of a magazine my housemaid would read. This is the Army we're dealing with, not a handful of Bolsheviks. I really need something more ... conclusive.

MAHLER.   *(Impassive.)* The graffiti all over the city walls, last month. That was them too. We're looking for the paint and stencils. Would *that* satisfy you?

MOHR.   Me, Mahler? It's got nothing to do with me. It's *proper procedure.* Considering the people involved. If this gets out it should be an open and shut case. Or it should be quietly dismissed. *(Mahler starts to object, changes his mind, salutes and exits. Mohr lights up the hundredth cigarette. Lights change. Up above we see Probst and Graf enter flanked by two Gestapo men. They stop at a table and empty their pockets. As they are escorted to separate cells, the Gestapo men exit. War planes fly past. Cell doors clang shut.)*

DAY 2 — FRIDAY, FEBRUARY 19, 1943

> *Lights up in Mohr's office. Sophie and Mohr are seated face to face. It's very early in the morning.*

MOHR.   Listen, Sophie. I'm an understanding man. I have a daughter your age, who — Believe me, all young people object to their government at one time or another. In fact I find it odd when they don't. And then they grow up, and —
SOPHIE.   They ... what?
MOHR.   They *grow up!*... *(The church bells outside toll five times.)* They join society, and get on with their lives. All this talk about high moral action —
SOPHIE.   Sometimes high moral action is the only way to avoid going mad.
MOHR.   Bullshit! Look, if you come clean with me, I'm sure we can arrange things. There are workcamps for — *(Sophie has been rubbing her forehead with the back of her hand.)* What is it?
SOPHIE.   Nothing. A headache. I get headaches.
MOHR.   Really? I get them too. Here. *(He takes an aspirin from his desk drawer and pours her a glass of water from a decanter. Sophie takes both. While she drinks, Mohr wipes his brow and loosens his tie.)* They can be hereditary, they tell me. Does your father get them? Mine did.
SOPHIE.   I don't think so.
MOHR.   Your father's first name is —
SOPHIE.   Robert.
MOHR.   Ah, yes, Robert. Like me. *(Beat.)* Do you like him?
SOPHIE.   Yes!
MOHR.   That's good. *(Pause.)* Do you have a dog? I have a dog. Bismarck.
SOPHIE.   A doberman?

29

MOHR.   A terrier. Doesn't like anybody but me.

SOPHIE.   Mine is called Freddie. He's a mutt. He likes everybody. He follows parades. *(Beat.)* He's quite busy these days. *(They unexpectedly burst out laughing. Then.)* Do you like your job? *(Silence.)*

MOHR.   *(Abruptly.)* About your brother's friends —

SOPHIE.   We have the same friends.

MOHR.   Including Christoph Probst?

SOPHIE.   *(Nervous.)* Why, yes, we know Christoph.

MOHR.   We've just arrested a Christoph Probst —

SOPHIE.   No!

MOHR.   — who claims he doesn't know you very well. In fact, he claims exclusive responsibility —

SOPHIE.   He knows nothing about it! *(Pause.)*

MOHR.   About what, Sophie? *(No answer. Blackout. Lights up in the studio. Hans, Schmorell, Sophie, Probst, Willi.)* Mid-argument.

HANS.   We've made effective contacts in Hamburg, Salzburg, Linz and Vienna!

SCHMORELL.   Augsburg and Stuttgart this week, too. There is response everywhere!

PROBST.   How much response?

HANS.   We've friends in three other universities already reproducing and passing on leaflets. That scum'll think this is a nation-wide movement. When we get to the Resistance —

PROBST.   The Resistance won't come out of hiding just because somebody wrote a few pamphlets!

HANS.   People are outraged at Stalingrad. All those dead boys.... They have families.... Men wearing party badges have been attacked in the streets. It's only a matter of time.

PROBST.   I don't know.

SOPHIE.   Chris ... if you don't want to —

PROBST.   Of course I want to ... I'm going to be a doctor. I'll be taking an oath about saving lives. What else can I do?

SCHMORELL.   Perhaps nothing. You have a wife and two children.

PROBST.   "Nothing" is not an option.

HANS. We'll stop them, Chris. The entire youth of Germany will rise and send that rabble back to the sewer it crawled out of.

PROBST. Are we swashbuckling? Is that what we're doing?

SCHMORELL. Come on, Chris! There's nothing like a little swashbuckling to brighten things up, I always say.

PROBST. Aren't you ever afraid, Alex?

SCHMORELL. Oh, yes. But they'll never know it when — *if* we get caught.

WILLI. *(Smiling.)* God's on our side. We can't get caught.

PROBST. Oh, Willi. Do you think of this as some kind of — 12th century Crusade?

WILLI. *(Very simply.)* I am a practicing Catholic. I believe every article of the faith. I cannot even pretend to support National Socialism ...

PROBST. Alex?

SCHMORELL. Oh, I believe in ... I don't know, the Sistine Chapel, the *Ninth Symphony*, Stradivarius ...

ALL. *(Ragging him.)* ... Frank Sinatra ...

SOPHIE. I'm taking two thousand to Frankfurt tomorrow.

PROBST. Careful on the train.

SOPHIE. Always.

SCHMORELL. What time?

SOPHIE. Nine.

SCHMORELL. And don't talk to anybody, that way nobody will remember you.

SOPHIE. Oh, nobody notices me anyway.

SCHMORELL. Impossible. *(They look at each other.)* You always wear a flower in your hair.

SOPHIE. *(Patting it.)* For good luck.

SCHMORELL. Flowers bring good luck?

SOPHIE. It's a well-known fact.

HANS. Sophie, your little world is governed by the most mysterious laws.

SOPHIE. My world is enormous! *(Hans and Probst start putting leaflets in stacks. Schmorell, after a moment's hesitation walks over to Sophie.)*

SCHMORELL. Sophie, would you like to — *(There is a knock*

on the door.)

V.O.   Curfew and blackout in five minutes!

WILLI.   I've to go. I need the batch for Salzburg.

PROBST.   And I'm going back to Innsbruck tomorrow morning, so I'll take mine now too. *(Willi and Probst stuff their satchels with leaflets.)*

HANS.   You don't have to —

PROBST.   *I want to.*

WILLI.   Does that look all right? They're not too bulky?

HANS.   For God's sake, don't drop it.

SOPHIE.   Remember, on the train, put the satchels on an overhead rack far away from where you're sitting.

PROBST.   Right.

SCHMORELL.   Put them near some pig with a party badge.

HANS.   And look stupid.

SCHMORELL.   Last time I looked stupid the S.A. tried to recruit me.

PROBST.   See you in a week or so. God willing. Come along, Willi.

WILLI.   Right. Good-bye!

SOPHIE.   Be careful!

HANS.   Good-bye! Don't put them all in the same mailbox!

SOPHIE.   And look carefully all around before you slip them in.

WILLI.   "Careful." *(Laughing.)* Funny word for us to use.

HANS.   And remember the code!

PROBST.   Right. The chorus of the Beethoven Ninth.

HANS.   *Whistled.*

WILLI.   What?

HANS.   It's got to be whistled. You hear that and you get the hell out. It means they're close. *(Willi can't do it. They demonstrate. Willi still can't do it.)*

PROBST.   Christ. I hope *you* never have to use it. *(Willi and Probst exit ad-libbing good-byes, etc., Willi still whistling piteously down the hall.)*

SCHMORELL.   Well, what shall we do? The night is young.

HANS.   Well, we could —

SOPHIE.   We've some more printing to do.

HANS/SCHMORELL.   What? No!

SOPHIE.   Just another couple of thousand. For Ulm!

HANS.   I want to go out by the river, cool a bottle of wine in the water, talk to girls about verses and sonatas and jazz and the moon ... and ... all that ...

SOPHIE.   Yes, well, I'd like to go dancing, but we can't do that anymore ...

SCHMORELL.   Why not?

SOPHIE.   There isn't ... enough time. Let's get to work.

SCHMORELL.   We'll be here all night!

SOPHIE.   I can't stand it when men whine. *(As they start getting the machine ready, an air raid siren is heard.)*

HANS.   Damn!

SCHMORELL.   Go to the shelter, Sophie, we'll take care of this.

SOPHIE.   Oh, for God's sake! We've a lot to do. Come on! *(As they start printing the air raid begins. They turn off most of the lights and they print lit by the bomb blasts. At times they huddle together on the floor, but they keep on cranking the machine. Schmorell gets a pair of binoculars and tries to look through a chink in the blacked out window.)*

SCHMORELL.   Damn, they keep missing Gestapo headquarters!

HANS.   It's the RAF, they're being polite, old boy.

SOPHIE.   We don't need "polite." I say blast the bastards!

HANS/SCHMORELL.   *(Startled.)* Sophie!

SOPHIE.   Get away from that window and print!

SCHMORELL.   Who says we have no time? Sophie, did you say you want to dance?

SOPHIE.   What?

SCHMORELL.   This is *our* time. This is the time we have. Do you want to dance?

SOPHIE.   *(Shouting over the bombs.)* Music! There's no music!

SCHMORELL.   Then we'll have to make some. *(He grabs Sophie around the waist and starts singing the* Wiener Blut Waltz *as he dances with her around the room. Sophie laughs and sings along.)* Louder! *(Hans joins them singing as he takes over the printer from Sophie. Sophie and Schmorell continue to dance, Hans prints and the bombs fall as music wells up and the lights fade to black.)*

DAY 3 — SATURDAY, FEBRUARY 20, 1943

Lights up on Mohr's office. Mahler bursts in.

MAHLER.   We've got them. The whole lot of them. We have the reports from the second team.   We found the mimeograph machine, a typewriter, paper! Also the stencils and the oil paint. There's enough evidence to incriminate an army.

MOHR.   As long as it's not ours, Mahler.

MAHLER.   *(Beat.)* The typewriter and mimeograph machine have been traced to an Alexander Schmorell, a close friend of the Scholls, also a —

MOHR.   — a *medic* in the Second Student Company?

MAHLER.   Why, yes. *(Beat.)* We have men out looking for him. Sir, I think we've uncovered a large network of agent-provocateurs and underground agitators, most likely in the pay of foreign powers. They must have connections everywhere.

MOHR.   In a way I hope you're right, Mahler. Because if this turns out to be the work of a handful of college students ...

MAHLER.   Then the case will have to be closed immediately.

MOHR.   I quite agree. Get the little bastards off to the front where they belong and out of here so we can do our job.

MAHLER.   Oh, no, no. Quite the contrary, you see. *Our job* is to handle it ... quickly, that's all. *(Mohr looks at him.)* Quickly. Efficiently. Surely you understand.... So as not to look too terribly foolish. *(Pause. Mohr presses the buzzer.)*

MOHR.   Well, they're not my problem. I'm signing papers for their immediate transfer to the appropriate military authorities.

MAHLER.   Like the *previous* Munich Gestapo, the Army has a history of leniency with their own, sir. *(Bauer enters.)*

MOHR.   *(Surprised.)* What are you doing here at this time of night? Where's Hofmann?

BAUER. Out sick, sir. Ate something bad.

MOHR. *(Beat.)* Get Sophie Scholl back in here. *(Bauer exits.)* Now Mahler, the civil authorities have no jurisdiction over members of the Armed forces. To risk friction between the High Command and the Reich Ministry of Justice at this time would be extremely problematic.

MAHLER. I don't think Berlin wants a military tribunal.

MOHR. Herr Mahler: I am a police officer. I don't deal in politics and I don't handle Army matters. I have cases of sabotage, arson, war-profiteering, air-raid looting and attempted assassination in my hands. Troubled waters stir up scum. I'm after scum. I don't have time to deal with adolescents wailing about the "power of the spirit," *AND I DON'T CLEAN HOUSE FOR THE WEHRMACHT!* I want these people out of here! *(Pause.)*

MAHLER. And the girl, sir?

MOHR. I believe I've made myself clear about the girl. You can go home, Mahler. I won't be needing you.

MAHLER. Sir, I'd rather —

MOHR. *(Pointedly.)* I don't need you. Heil Hitler. *(Mahler starts to exit and has to hold the door open for Bauer and Sophie. She's in a nightgown with her coat over it. She's been gotten out of bed. At the door, Mahler and Sophie face each other for a second. She instinctively recoils and enters. Mohr dismisses Bauer with a gesture.)* Several of your connections with other universities have been arrested.

SOPHIE. *Connections?* I have school friends. We're not political.

MOHR. We're at war. That statement is not acceptable.

SOPHIE. *(Fighting sleep and fear.)* I don't believe in war.

MOHR. *(Quickly closing the door.)* And that statement can put you in prison for life.

SOPHIE. Should I lie to you?

MOHR. You've been lying to me for two days.

SOPHIE. I don't know what you mean.

MOHR. What exactly is your relationship to Christoph Probst, Alexander Schmorell, and Wilhelm Graf?

SOPHIE. We study together, we have parties ...

MOHR. *Printing* parties?

SOPHIE. I don't know what you mean.

MOHR. Do you understand what an accusation of high treason means? *(Silence.)* What is your relationship to Professor Huber?

SOPHIE. Huber?

MOHR. Kurt Huber, yes.

SOPHIE. Oh. I took his course. Introduction to philosophy.

MOHR. Did your brother take his course too?

SOPHIE. He ... may have.

MOHR. You took his course together, very recently.

SOPHIE. I'd forgotten.

MOHR. As a matter of fact, all of you have taken that course at one time or another.

SOPHIE. *(Shrugging.)* He's good.

MOHR. But a few moments ago you had trouble remembering his name.

SOPHIE. I don't know what you mean.

MOHR. That seems to be your favorite statement.

SOPHIE. I'm sorry.

MOHR. *(Picking up some leaflets.)* Just how good a teacher is he? Is he the one who fed you all this *cant*?

SOPHIE. I don't ... what?

MOHR. What is his particular attraction? Why does he have so many students?

SOPHIE. *(Pause.)* He is an extremely patriotic man. These are hard times. He is adamant about — the preservation of German honor.

MOHR. What's his opinion on the Führer?

SOPHIE. *(Very politely.)* He never mentions the Führer in connection to German honor. *(Beat.)* It's an introductory course, you know ... the Greeks and all that ... Plato, Socrates, —

MOHR. What about the seventeenth century?

SOPHIE. Some.

MOHR. Spinoza, for instance?

SOPHIE. Spinoza?

MOHR. Spinoza: the Jew.

SOPHIE.   Oh, yes. Professor Huber told us we are not to read him.

MOHR.   It seems he spent the better part of a week telling you not to read him. *And* Sigmund Freud!

SOPHIE.   *(Impenetrable.)* He was explaining how dangerous they are.

MOHR.   *(Beat.)* We know that this Professor Huber has — *had*, little soirées, to which his "favorite" pupils were invited and where certain topics were discussed.

SOPHIE.   I've never heard of them.

MOHR.   I suppose your brother and his friends haven't either?

SOPHIE.   We don't go to a lot of parties.

MOHR.   But you said you did.

SOPHIE.   What?

MOHR.   You said you had "parties" together, just a moment ago.

SOPHIE.   I ... what?

MOHR.   With your friends. You said you had parties with your friends.

SOPHIE.   Oh.... But not with —

MOHR.   Not with the "Professor." I see.

SOPHIE.   No.

MOHR.   Not even to discuss the "preservation of German Honor," whatever that may mean?

SOPHIE.   You don't know what it means?

MOHR.   It depends on whose terms.

SOPHIE.   Honor has no terms. It's the one thing in life that's absolute.

MOHR.   Then surely you can explain to me what it is.

SOPHIE.   I wouldn't presume to explain to a government official what German honor is ... or should be.

MOHR.   I wouldn't find it presumptuous. I'd find it interesting. Please.

SOPHIE.   I don't know the difference between personal honor and national honor. Do you? *(Pause.)*

MOHR.   *(Abruptly.)* What about boys, Sophie. Aren't you in love? *(Sophie starts involuntarily.)* Are you in love, Sophie? *(She looks at him.*) What about your parents? Are you fond of them?

SOPHIE. *Fond?* I wouldn't say "fond." "Fond" is a sentimental notion.

MOHR. Think very carefully. Could you not have been influenced by the wrong sort of people ... let us say, a subversive element in our universities, and misled into doing something the implications of which you did not understand? Students, especially young women, are often impressionable, easily confused. This "professor" of yours could turn out to be the only one responsible —

SOPHIE. I don't understand. But, as you say, I'm a *girl*, and *girls* are easily confused.

MOHR. Damn it! Don't try to turn the tables on me Sophie, I'm an old hand at this!

SOPHIE. I don't think so.

MOHR. What?!

SOPHIE. I think you're rather new at this. And you don't like it.

MOHR. *(Exploding.)* What in hell — Do you not want to live?

SOPHIE. Passionately!

MOHR. Passion is for the Opera, Sophie, not for everyday life.

SOPHIE. Too bad for everyday life. *(Pause.)*

MOHR. Look, it's time you went back to your ...

SOPHIE. Cell? That word doesn't come easily to you. *(Gently.)* You must be in the wrong business.

MOHR. *(Snapping.)* Serving Germany is not a business. It's a privilege.

SOPHIE. You love Germany?

MOHR. What? Certainly, I —

SOPHIE. Because I love Germany ... passionately. *(Pause.)*

MOHR. Bauer! *(Bauer enters.)* Get me Mahler right away.

BAUER. Yes, sir. *(Bauer exits.)*

MOHR. *(To Sophie.)* I'll be calling you again.

SOPHIE. I expect you will.

MOHR. *(Looking through his papers.)* Good day.

SOPHIE. I wish it were. *(Sophie exits escorted by Bauer who opens the door for her and gives her a long vacant look. Mohr goes to his desk abruptly and takes out an aspirin or two which he takes very quickly with a glass of water. He paces the room.)*

MOHR.   Goddamnit! *(Mahler enters, papers in hand.)* I want the complete dossier for this case and Colonels Hauser and Dohrn on the phone immediately.

MAHLER.   Sir: the Reich Minister of Justice and the High Command have temporarily agreed to suspend restrictions on Civil jurisdiction over the military.

MOHR.   *(Stunned.)* At this time of night?

MAHLER.   They've been discharged and turned over to us — uh, the Ministry of Justice. *(Beat.)* They're already out of uniform, sir.

MOHR.   On whose orders?

MAHLER.   Berlin, sir.

MOHR.   Then Berlin can have them!!

MAHLER.   They would like it handled in Munich, sir.

MOHR.   Do "they" also want us to tell the nation and the world at large that the Armed Forces of the Third Reich and the Hitler Youth together have produced an element which publicly calls for the downfall of this government? Because I warn you, the BBC is going to have a field day with this!

MAHLER.   That's precisely why —

MOHR.   This is an Army scandal and they want to put it on us, don't you see?

MAHLER.   There won't be a scandal, sir.

MOHR.   When the public —

MAHLER.   There will be no public, sir.

MOHR.   Do you imagine we can cover this up?

MAHLER.   There's an official press blackout on the case. The People's Court is travelling from Berlin tonight. They will be in Munich in 24 hours. The trial has been set for Monday morning at ten. Dr. Roland Freisler is presiding. *(Beat.)* It'll go very quickly. *(A silence.)*

MOHR.   You've been very busy, Mahler.

MAHLER.   Thank you, sir. May we expect the indictments first thing tomorrow? *(Pause. Through the glass pane Bauer's shadow is seen slowly pacing.)*

MOHR.   The nature of the indictments will depend upon the information collected. And they will be handed over when *all* the evidence is in my hands ... to my satisfaction. Which means that, as all allegations seem largely circumstantial at the moment and are not corroborated except by the ... by this *Herr Schmidt*, I will need something along the lines of a confession.

MAHLER.   What?!

MOHR.   A confession, Mahler. To hand to the public at some point, should the Press, in an over-zealous attempt to uphold the system, commit an indiscretion.

MAHLER.   *(Beat.)* Will there be anything else, sir?

MOHR.   *(Rising.)* Yes, Mahler. All action concerning this case must be initiated or approved by me, *before* it's carried out. I want interrogation to proceed carefully and all information to pass through my desk before it is forwarded anywhere else. Under no circumstances should there be any contact with news agencies of any kind, or, for that matter, with other departments of the government, until I decide it's appropriate. That will be all. *(They look at each other. Mahler salutes and exits. Mohr paces. Bauer enters with dossier and puts it on the desk.)*

BAUER.   The papers, sir. Will there be anything else, sir?

MOHR.   *(Going through the dossier.)* Half — half a dozen — bookish — students. And a duplicating machine. A mimeograph. No, no weapons, no gunpowder, no nitroglycerine. No home-made bombs. They've taken on the Third Reich with ... an old typewriter, some paper and a printing machine.

BAUER.   Yes, sir.

MOHR.   Son-of-a-bitch! *(To himself.)* Dropping the goddamn things all over the ... *(He trails off.)* Stupid, stupid ... stupid ...

BAUER.   Bad business, sir. When our very own people —

MOHR.   Put my car back in the garage. I'm not going home.

BAUER.   Yes, sir. *(Bauer turns to go.)*

MOHR.   What's it all about? What difference will it make? *(Bauer stops at the door and turns to look at him. The bells from the Frauenkirche are heard. U., directly behind Mohr, Hans and Sophie are seen running up a flight of stairs, reaching the top and flinging*

*an armful of white sheets of paper into the air in a triumphant ges-
ture. Chopin's* Grande Polonaise in E Flat Major *fills the house.
Mohr closes his eyes.)* What the hell difference will it —

Blackout

END OF ACT ONE

ACT TWO

It's late night. Hans, Willi, and Schmorell are discovered painting anti-Nazi graffiti on the walls of the city. Large greenish letters that say "Freedom!," "Down with Hitler!," "Hitler, mass murderer!." Visible upstage center is an enormous swastika which has been crossed out. They work fast, with one flashlight which they keep covering every time they think they hear a noise. Police sirens are heard intermittently in the distance. Once in a while they explode in muffled laughter. Two paint, one stands guard. Suddenly they hear a very distinct whistle of somebody walking by, which, as it gets closer can be identified as the "Ode to Joy" from the Beethoven Ninth.

HANS. Let's go!
SCHMORELL. Shit! *(The flashlight goes out and they hide in the shadows. A night patrol can be heard coming very close. Voices are heard and harsh bright lights flood the stage for a moment, barely missing the freshly painted wall. Routine check. The lights go out, the patrol can be heard passing them by.)*
WILLI. Come on! *(They run off. Lights up in Hans's rooms. Hans, Probst, Sophie, Schmorell. Tumult in the streets. Willi storms in out of breath.)* Student riot!
SOPHIE. Where?
WILLI. The university! Right now! Let's —
PROBST. What happened?
WILLI. At the war support rally. The goon they sent to speak to us was more than usually repulsive and he went too far! He said women were "for breedin' not for schoolin', and if some of you ladies don't have the looks to find your own men, I'll be glad to offer you some of mine. At the very least, I can promise you a good time!" All hell broke loose! The girls in the gallery started booing, and they tried to arrest

them and the boys stood up for them. They're throwing SA and Gestapo men out the windows! It took me ten minutes to get out of there. It's great!

HANS. A student demonstration! They've done it! Finally!

SOPHIE. And *the girls* started it? And we weren't there?

HANS. *(To Probst.)* What did I tell you? Come on, let's go!

PROBST. Wait! Where are they? Are they inside?

WILLI. Some have taken to the streets; they're heading for Gestapo headquarters! It's happening! It's really happening! *(Suddenly police sirens are heard in the distance. They gradually become very loud. Gun fire begins.)*

PROBST. Riot Police.

SOPHIE. No!

HANS. Damn it.

PROBST. What did you expect? *(The sounds of shots, marching boots, trucks, sirens in the streets.)*

SCHMORELL. Let's go give a hand! *(There is a knock on the door. Everybody freezes.)*

V.O. Scholl, telephone!

HANS. Who in hell — Wait for me. *(Hans goes out. The sounds of battle outside increase.)*

SCHMORELL. I'm going out. Take a look.

SOPHIE. Alex, don't.

SCHMORELL. We'll keep a safe distance. If we can do anything, we'll — jump in, if not — we won't. I'm not crazy.

WILLI. Coming. *(Willi and Alex exit. Probst goes to the window.)*

PROBST. I can't see anything.

SOPHIE. I'm going to get my coat. *(Hans returns, obviously disturbed.)*

HANS. Shit!

SOPHIE. What is it?

HANS. The signal again.

SOPHIE. What signal?

HANS. The whistling. The Beethoven.

PROBST. Again? Who can it be?

HANS. They were in a hurry. Public phone. I heard the whistling and they hung up.

SOPHIE. Somebody wants us to stay away. To ... stop ... for

a while.

HANS. *(Pause.)* Or we could do something so incredibly bold as to shake the whole nation.

PROBST. Are you crazy? Somebody knows who we are! Somebody *in there* knows who we are!

HANS. *(Not listening.)* Something that would be like a great blaze of light across the sky calling all the decent people of Germany to action.

PROBST. There may not be any decent people left in Germany.

HANS. That's not true! Look at today!

PROBST. *(At window.)* It's awfully quiet out there all of a sudden.

SOPHIE. People are good. They're just frightened.

PROBST. Where are they, Sophie, where are they?

SOPHIE. They were in the streets a moment ago!

PROBST. A handful, just like us. The rest are silent.

SOPHIE. *(Desperate.)* They're waiting!

PROBST. How in hell can you be so sure?

HANS. Don't you want to find out?

PROBST. We mustn't commit any desperate acts. *(Willi and Schmorell return.)*

SCHMORELL. It's over.

WILLI. They've — stopped it.

SOPHIE. And the students?

SCHMORELL. They're arresting everybody. And worse. *(Pause.)*

HANS. *(Shaken.)* Who's desperate? Let's get something to eat.

SCHMORELL. There's something else, Hans.

HANS. What?

SCHMORELL. The people. They shut their doors when the riot police went after the students in the streets. Nobody would let them in. *(Pause.)*

HANS. They're scared. They're just scared. They're waiting. *(Pause.)* How — how's the new baby? *(Probst pulls out pictures, as always.)*

SOPHIE. Oh, Chris, he's so pretty!

SCHMORELL.   Three kids now?
PROBST.   *(Quietly.)* Three. *(They all look at him. Blackout.)*

DAY 4 — SUNDAY, FEBRUARY 21, 1943

> *Lights up on Sophie and Mohr. Sunday morning. They've been up all night.*

MOHR.   Do you know the whereabouts of Alexander Schmorell? *(No answer.)* There is nothing to be afraid of. I know you're not directly involved. *(Pause.)*
SOPHIE.   I have to tell you something.
MOHR.   All you need to tell me is where to find Schmorell.
SOPHIE.   You're very wrong about me.
MOHR.   Stop!
SOPHIE.   It was —
MOHR.   No! Just the others. Tell me about the others —
SOPHIE.   The others are —
MOHR.   Don't —
SOPHIE.   ... me.
MOHR.   *(Overlapping.)* — do that!! *(Silence. Mohr turns away from her.)* Of all the stupid —
SOPHIE.   Isn't that what you wanted? *(Silence.)* What *do* you want Herr Mohr?
MOHR.   I'm going to give you a chance to reconsider your statement.
SOPHIE.   Why?
MOHR.   I'm giving you a choice, goddamn it!
SOPHIE.   The moment of choice is past. I never felt so alive in my whole life. Nothing will ever feel like that again.
MOHR.   The only way to avoid disappointment is to die young!
SOPHIE.   *(Lightly.)* They say if you die young, you trick death. You live forever.
MOHR.   You hold yourself in high regard.
SOPHIE.   I must. God made me.
MOHR.   Then he must have made me too.

SOPHIE. *(Pause.)* It all comes out right in the end.

MOHR. Really. *(Pause.)* Why did you call yourselves "The White Rose?"

SOPHIE. *(Beat.)* Haven't you ever seen one? *(Silence.)*

MOHR. A fragile flower, my wife says. Can't keep them longer than a day. *(Beat.)* That's all, thank you. *(She rises and exits. Blackout. Lights up on Hans and Sophie. A street. Hans carries a small suitcase. Schmorell enters.)*

SCHMORELL. Where are you off to?

SOPHIE. School.

SCHMORELL. It's Thursday. You don't have classes on Thursday.

HANS. *(Shows him his suitcase.)* Business.

SCHMORELL. *(Pause.)* In the middle of the day? That's dangerous. Why?

HANS. It needs to be done.

SCHMORELL. At the University? Hans, that's too close.

HANS. It's time. They're ready.

SCHMORELL. I wouldn't —

HANS. That student riot was the first public protest in years. They're ready. If it's going to happen, it's going to happen at the university. I know it.

SCHMORELL. *(Beat.)* All right, I'm coming with you.

HANS. No.

SCHMORELL. Why not?

HANS. Three's too many. *(Laughs.)* We're going to look like a delegation.

SCHMORELL. Remember we're taking the early Berlin train tomorrow morning. People are counting on us. If you start something at school —

HANS. Will Harnack be at the station?

SCHMORELL. Yes. We're meeting the others at his apartment. Man called Bonhoeffer, a clergyman, and somebody from the Army. And someone from Italy!

HANS. How did he get a passport?

SCHMORELL. Got himself invited to lecture on Renaissance Art.

SOPHIE. A contact with the resistance, finally! *(An awkward*

46

pause.)

SCHMORELL.   Do we celebrate ... tonight?

HANS.   Of course. The studio, around eight?

SCHMORELL.   Fine. I've a good bottle of wine. Don't — do anything I wouldn't do. *(They laugh.)*

SOPHIE.   We have to go.

SCHMORELL.   *(Suddenly.)* Sophie, wait.

SOPHIE.   What is it?

SCHMORELL.   *(Beat.)* Don't go!

SOPHIE.   *(Gently.)* What?

SCHMORELL.   *(Desperate.)* Don't go! Stay with me! It's such a beautiful day. Let's go for a walk! We'll feed the pigeons in the plaza, buy a new ribbon for your hair, read sonnets on a park bench, see a movie ... and tonight, we go dancing. *(She looks at him.)* Right. Got something for you. *(He pulls a little wild flower from his pocket.)* For good luck. *(Sophie takes the flower and puts it behind her ear. Hans turns away.)*

SOPHIE.   It's going to be a good day. *(Sophie kisses him lightly on the cheek and walks away very fast with Hans. Schmorell watches them go. He walks off whistling his Wiener Blut Waltz. A second whistling is heard mingling with Schmorell's who stops. The other person is whistling the Beethoven Ninth.)*

SCHMORELL.   Who's there?... Who's there?... Who are you? *(The whistling of the Beethoven Ninth fades away as we hear footsteps moving away. Cross fade with lights up on Mohr and Mahler.)*

MAHLER.   Alexander Schmorell has just turned himself in, sir. They're all here. We can begin indict—

MOHR.   Shaeffer wants extensive information. Monday's too soon.

MAHLER.   The Assize Court, room 216 is reserved for tomorrow.

MOHR.   *(Beat.)* Provided the indictments are ready.

MAHLER.   I beg your pardon, sir?

MOHR.   I said *provided* the indictments are ready. And *I* am in charge of the indictments, Mahler. *(Deliberately.)* They're not ready.

MAHLER.   It's been four days now and —

MOHR.   Dr. Freisler is going to need a properly documented case.

MAHLER. What?

MOHR. He's going to want a properly documented case.

MAHLER. Since when?!

MOHR. Come again?

MAHLER. *(Angry for the first time.)* Since when does the People's Court require extensive documentation of the kind —

MOHR. *(Rising.)* Herr Mahler, are you officially alleging that Dr. Roland Freisler and the People's Court are in the habit of proceeding without sufficient proof?

MAHLER. What? Of course not! I only —

MOHR. Then certainly you cannot object to my protecting the Court's best interests by furnishing them with the necessary evidence. That could be considered *obstructive.* I would be forced to report that sort of thing to my superiors *in Berlin.*

MAHLER. That's not what I —

MOHR. Allied propaganda has it that we're ... rotting from the inside ... Dr. Goebbels doesn't want another army scandal on the front page and I agree with him. Because this can go very wrong, if we're not careful. *(Pause.)*

MAHLER. It's a clear-cut case, sir —

MOHR. *(Exploding.)* Goddamn it you're beginning to sound like those kids, Mahler! *Nothing* is clear-cut. There is a war going on! Ordinary solutions do not apply! Ordinary measures do not apply! Ordinary thinking does not apply! Bauer! *(Bauer enters immediately.)* Bring me that girl again.

BAUER. Yes, sir.

MOHR. *(To Mahler.)* You start with Schmorell. *(Bauer exits. Mahler holds for a beat and follows him out.)* Damn! *(He reads from the White Rose leaflets.)* "Spirit," "moral duty!," "cowardice" ... where the hell do they get — what am I supposed to — what am I sup — *(Church bells toll the hour outside. He looks for his pocket watch, remembers he doesn't have it.)* Time. Time. There's no more time. *(Blackout. Lights up on Mahler and Schmorell. The following will be a "montage" of interrogation scenes with all five prisoners involved. It will be effected with cross lighting to emphasize speed and tension.)*

SCHMORELL.   I understand you have some dreary people called Scholl here? I suggest you release them at once if you don't wish to appear too ridiculous. All they know is applestrudel and church. They're from Ulm. I used the studio alone.

MAHLER.   They've confessed, Schmorell. You're too late. You see, you didn't have to turn yourself in after all. *(Silence.)*

SCHMORELL.   Ah, well. All this on the word of a ... *Jakob Schmidt?*

MAHLER.   If you will sign here, I'll take your admission of —

SCHMORELL.   Guilt? A Freudian, eh? Oh, sorry. I'm not signing anything without my father's attorneys present. Has he been contacted by the way?

MAHLER.   You don't really expect all that money to protect you from prosecution and conviction?

SCHMORELL.   Careful, Herr Mahler. That remark reeks of Bolshevism. *(Pause.)*

MAHLER.   Where were you on the morning of February 18?

SCHMORELL.   What year?

MAHLER.   *(Unruffled.)* 1943.

SCHMORELL.   Why don't you ask the janitor?

MAHLER.   Does the name "The White Rose" mean anything to you?

SCHMORELL.   I'm not all that keen on gardening. The staff does that at home.

MAHLER.   You think you're going to get away with this because you're all members of "respectable" Aryan families?

SCHMORELL.   I'm half Russian, you know. Who knows what perverted Slavic blood might have seeped into me in the womb.

MAHLER.   You consider yourself an outsider?

SCHMORELL.   If you mean someone who becomes the creator of his own world and not a mere inhabitant, you mean an artist. I don't have the talent.

MAHLER.   Or a "resistance" fighter.

SCHMORELL.   *German* resistance? That's a contradiction in terms.

MAHLER. You know, Schmorell, you are the perfect example of a mind distorted by what you, intellectuals, like to call "culture."

SCHMORELL. Actually, I prefer running about in skins, grunting and rubbing sticks to make fire. The only difficulty is that the knuckles tend to get a bit raw. *(Lights on Mohr and Sophie.)*

SOPHIE. For Germany.

MOHR. Germany is the Third Reich.

SOPHIE. *(Furious.)* No! She's the Hessian Forests, Goethe, Mendelssohn, the sun setting on the Rhine, God.

MOHR. *(Quickly.)* There is no God.

SOPHIE. That may very well be, but there is the *idea* of God. And like most ideas, it far surpasses reality ... as we know it. *(Lights come up on another part of the stage on Willi Graf and Mahler.)*

WILLI. My faith expressly forbids all involvement direct or indirect with the destruction of any and all human life.

MAHLER. Come on, man! Thousands of Roman Catholics have fought countless wars and slaughtered countless people!

WILLI. I cannot account for others, sir. I can only answer for myself.

MAHLER. Who is at the head of the so-called White Rose operation?

WILLI. *(Beat.)* I am.

MAHLER. Does your "faith" allow you to lie?

WILLI. *(Beat.)* I would have to discuss that with a Jesuit father.

MAHLER. Are you receiving orders from abroad?

WILLI. We receive no orders, sir. From anybody.

MAHLER. Where did the money come from?

WILLI. Our personal allowances from home. *(Apologetic.)* That's why the quality of the paper is not so good.

MAHLER. Are you going to tell me you did this all by yourselves?

WILLI. I did it. I set it all up.

MAHLER. How?

WILLI. How? *(He panics.)* Well, you know ... it wasn't easy!

MAHLER. I see. Why, Graf?

WILLI. Because there comes a time when you can't continue to be blown about by whatever wind may come your way. One must make a free choice. It's the Christian, the human thing to do.

MAHLER. Christian?

WILLI. Free will. We have it. We must exercise it.

MAHLER. This is all about ... God?

WILLI. Or honor. I don't know which. I can't tell them apart. *(Lights fade on Willi and Mahler and come up on Mohr and Probst.)*

PROBST. We are specifically referring to acts of aggression perpetrated against German citizens —

MOHR. The Reich does not commit acts of aggression against its lawful citizens when they remain within the law. That is Allied propaganda designed to undermine national morale.

PROBST. Then what *is* that large area enclosed in barbed wire and heavily guarded just off the road to Dachau? We happened on it one sunny day on our way home from the front.

MOHR. No doubt you are referring to a camp for political prisoners and prisoners of war, of which the Allies have several.

PROBST. And the yellow stars and pink triangles on the uniforms of these "prisoners of war," are they some sort of foreign war decoration?

MOHR. *(Exploding.)* Where do you think you are? Who do you think you're talking to? *(Cross fade and lights up on Schmorell and Mahler.)*

SCHMORELL. Don't make me answer that.

MAHLER. Under whose orders do you act?

SCHMORELL. *(Mysteriously.)* Very important people.

MAHLER. *(Alert.)* Important people?

SCHMORELL. *(Pointing upwards.)* Very ... high up. *(Mahler pulls out his little black notebook and pen from his pocket.)*

MAHLER. Foreign agents?

SCHMORELL. German.

MAHLER. Names.

SCHMORELL. Friedrich Schiller, Ludwig van Beethoven, Johannes Brahms, Thomas Aquinas, Heinrich —

MAHLER. *(Who had started writing.)* You're all full of "books" aren't you?

SCHMORELL. There are worse things to be full of, I dare say.

MAHLER. You talk like a Jew, Schmorell.

SCHMORELL. That's a relief. I was afraid I was getting a little too Teutonic for what's good for national culture.

MAHLER. Are you somehow under the impression that you are in a debate class at the University?

SCHMORELL. Nobody in their right mind would confuse Gestapo headquarters with a place of thought.

MAHLER. Schmorell, you are going before the People's Court on a charge of high treason. Do you know what that means?

SCHMORELL. It means that we will be tried on little or no evidence. The defense will be public-appointed and a sham, and there will be no press. The procedure will be merely a formality and we'll be convicted and sentenced to death. Tell me, will we be hanged or guillotined? *(Pause.)*

MAHLER. What is your relationship to Falk Harnack?

SCHMORELL. Never heard of him.

MAHLER. To Traute Lafrenz.

SCHMORELL. Don't know her.

MAHLER. Hans Leipelt?

SCHMORELL. Don't know him.

MAHLER. Albert Suhr.

SCHMORELL. Don't know him.

MAHLER. Most of these people have been arrested already. Why don't you cooperate?

SCHMORELL. *(Thinks for a moment.)* I know a Mathilde Schwarzkopf. *(Mahler starts writing. Cross fade and lights up on Mohr and Hans.)*

MOHR. Why didn't you run away? You're a good alpinist, you could have gone straight over to Switzerland.

HANS. *(Pause.)* I'm not the running away type.

MOHR.   Do you expect me to believe that?

HANS.   Herr Mohr, if you believe Hitler, you believe any-thing. The war is lost. It will be months before we come to trial, and months before the appeals and the final sentence go through. By then you will be a bad memory in history and the world will know that there were Germans who refused to live dishonorably. *(Pause.)*

MOHR.   The trial is set for tomorrow morning at ten. No appeals will be allowed and there will be no press ... of any kind. *(A silence. Mohr avoids eye contact.)*

HANS.   Who is the presiding judge?

MOHR.   *(With difficulty.)* Dr. Roland Freisler. For the People's Court.

HANS.   *(Pause.)* Why bother with a trial at all?

MOHR.   I don't know what you mean.

HANS.   Yes, you do. Freisler is a hanging judge, and the People's Court an indecent travesty.

MOHR.   *(Hollow.)* Dr. Freisler's an outstanding defender of —

HANS.   You are so uncomfortable with the truth, Herr Mohr.

MOHR.   Oh, what is "truth!"

HANS.   Pontius Pilate, John, 18.

MOHR.   *(Viciously.)* You have a death wish.

HANS.   A national German characteristic. I, however, am ra-bidly attached to life.

MOHR.   You were once in uniform. You've seen thousands of German soldiers die. How can you possibly turn against your country at a time like this?

HANS.   For the other German dead.

MOHR.   What other German dead?

HANS.   There are camps. Do you know what happens there?

MOHR.   I have nothing to do with that!

HANS.   We had neighbors. A family called Nathan. *Germans.* German nationals, Mohr. In Germany for generations. In fact, you couldn't get any more "German" than that. But you know something? They've disappeared! Nobody knows where they've gone. Their house is empty. Their door, boarded up. I want them back, Mohr. Can you do that? Can you find them for me? Because until I see the Nathans again, until I hear their piano, see their milk bottles at their doorstep; until I see them turning their lights on in the parlor, until then, I will hold *you* accountable!

MOHR.   Do you want to disappear with them? Is that going to help them?

HANS.   I want my neighbors back! I want my country back! Give me back my country, you son of a bitch! *(There is a pause during which Hans and Mohr stare at each other.)*

MOHR.   Bauer! *(Bauer enters.)* I am finished with the prisoner. *(Cross fade and lights up on Mahler and Willi.)*

MAHLER.   So. You *were* in foreign employ.

WILLI.   Well ... yes.

MAHLER.   Where are the headquarters of this organization?

WILLI.   ... In the Black Forest. Deep in the ... Black Forest.

MAHLER.   The Black Forest ... is a rather large area. Where exactly in the Black Forest?

WILLI.   Behind a wood-shed.

MAHLER.   *(Beat.)* Why don't we start at the beginning. *(As Willi leans forward on the table to talk, cross fade and lights up on Mohr and Sophie. It's pre-dawn.)*

MOHR.   Why, with everything to lose?

SOPHIE.   For me. I need to know who I am.

MOHR.   We're in the twentieth century, in the middle of a world war! That kind of individualism is outdated and out of place.

SOPHIE.   This is my time and this is my place.

MOHR.   *(Beat.)* Tell me, Sophie, these "fellow fighters of the resistance," these "young Germans," these friends, these "brothers" that the White Rose kept calling to arms, where are they? Have they answered? Have they come forth? Are they storming our doors to set you free? These German people who, as you say, "know the truth and what is decent and right," do you see them? Do you hear them? *(Pause.)*

SOPHIE.   They're afraid.

MOHR.   Yes, of you. People like their heroes nice and simple, Sophie. They like them to drop dead on the battlefield clutching a flag. They like the poor sods who die in their place ... *by chance, not by choice.* They're fondly remembered, and with great relief. "Thank God it wasn't me!" But you? People — *good people* — won't like you now or later. They'll think you arrogant, over-educated, and dangerous! And your worst enemy will be the honest man who will find his convictions — because he has convictions after all — getting in the way of his prosperity and will secretly think "who the hell did they think they were!" Fifty years from now school children in remote places of the world will know Adolph Hitler and will have never heard of Sophie Scholl. *(Pause.)*

SOPHIE.   I'm afraid. You're afraid. Life is frightening. That *sordid little man* in Berlin is no more frightening than life.

MOHR.   Do you imagine that you die for the good of humanity?

SOPHIE.   Life and death aren't transferrable. They are private affairs.

MOHR.   Ah yes. Very neat. Very neat. You must have read that somewhere, because it doesn't ring true. *Real.* It sounds like *literature.* Like something clever someone *writes* so people can quote it. Like the language in those goddamn pamphlets! I don't believe it. Real life doesn't turn out so *tidy.* So clean. Real life is messier. In *real* life, someone else always has to deal with your death. Pick up the pieces, as it were. *Clean up.*

SOPHIE.   Nobody —

MOHR.   Your parents, for instance.

SOPHIE.   What — ?

MOHR.   Your mother.

SOPHIE.   What about her?

MOHR.   Think about her. Not in the abstract. *Really think about her.*

SOPHIE.   I —

MOHR.   What was she wearing last time you saw her? When you went home. You *do* go home, don't you? When you're not printing pamphlets?

SOPHIE.   I don't —

MOHR.   What was she wearing? Answer me!

SOPHIE.   *(Almost inaudible.)* A — a blue —

MOHR. *(Walking away from her.)* What? I can't hear you!

SOPHIE. Blue sweater.

MOHR. Why?

SOPHIE. What?

MOHR. Why does she wear blue? Does she wear it often?

SOPHIE. *(Beat.)* Yes.

MOHR. Ah. She likes blue. Why, I wonder. Do you know? Are her eyes blue? *(Silence.)* Do you even know?

SOPHIE. Grey.

MOHR. What? I can't hear you!

SOPHIE. Grey!

MOHR. Ah. Grey. And your father? What's he like? What color are his eyes?

SOPHIE. I don't want to —

MOHR. Describe him to me. What are they like, these people who are going to have to clean up after you?

SOPHIE. I can't —

MOHR. Why not? After all he's just a man ... like me ...

SOPHIE. He's nothing like you! My father is nothing like you!

MOHR. Ah. Do you have his face now? Do you have his face right before you? In your mind? *(Silence.)* Will he survive your death do you think? And your brother's? Both of you at once. His son. His boy. Does he call him "my boy?" Fathers do that, you know. Think about him, Sophie, think hard. Think of them at breakfast, at lunch, at dinner. Think of him shaving, think of her cooking, ironing your clothes ... did you say she still does your laundry?

SOPHIE. I — I — don't —

MOHR. That's all, thank you. *(He turns his back on her. She slowly gets up to leave and at that moment the sun breaks through the night and floods the room. A bird starts singing. Sophie moves to the window and the room is bathed in golden light.)*

SOPHIE. A bird, singing in the dead of winter! What a beautiful day! It's so clear! Isn't life ... magnificent? *(She turns to him.)* Herr Mohr. I know you're not — Do you think ... is there a way ... that we might ... *live?* Isn't there a little ... back door ... a forgotten crack in the wall, a broken lock, a shattered window ... *anything* ... we could slip through? Perhaps nobody would notice. *(Pause. Mohr picks up his telephone and dials one number.)*

MOHR.   Fraulein Schweder? I want to dictate a statement for one of the suspects to sign. *(Cross fade and lights up on Mahler who is looking haggard and wan. He has notes scattered all over his table. Willi is rather flushed and animated.)*

MAHLER.   *Eisenhower* told you that?!

WILLI.   Yes ... well, not directly.

MAHLER.   Through an intermediary?

WILLI.   Yes!

MAHLER.   *(Exhausted.)* Name?

WILLI.   ... MacArthur.

MAHLER.   *General* MacArthur?!

WILLI.   Uh ... Corporal MacArthur.

MAHLER.   *(Pause.)* There is a *Corporal* MacArthur who acts as a go-between —

WILLI.   He's also my contact with Vishinski.

MAHLER.   Which Vishinski would that be?

WILLI.   The one in Moscow. *(Mahler gives up and stares ahead. Willi is exhilarated, if somewhat rattled. Blackout. Lights up on Mohr. He's pacing and smoking. A knock on the door.)*

MOHR.   Come in! *(Bauer enters.)* Yes, what — Don't you ever go home?

BAUER.   I — we're short handed, sir. Hofmann's still out. This came for you. *(Bauer hands him a note. Mohr reads it.)*

MOHR.   Dr. Freisler's here. Yes, Bauer, you seem to want to say something, if I read your expression correctly? I'm not always sure.

BAUER.   It's that girl, sir.

MOHR.   What about her?

BAUER.   She smuggled a cigarette to prisoner Graf, upstairs, sir. *(With a smirk.)* She scribbled the word "freedom" all over it, sir.

MOHR.   Thank you, Bauer. I don't think we should call the storm troopers just yet.

BAUER.   She's also using her water ration to ... for some ... thing — flower. To keep it alive.

MOHR. *(Exploding.)* I don't have the time to listen to drivel!

BAUER. *(Relentless.)* It's the prison guards, sir. They like them.

MOHR. What?

BAUER. Those kids. The guards like them. I don't know why. If you like, we could move them and I could take over —

MOHR. That won't be necessary Bauer.

BAUER. But I could —

MOHR. That will be all.

BAUER. *(Beat.)* Yes, sir. *(Bauer salutes, turns and exits crossing Mahler entering.)*

MAHLER. Goddamn waste of time! Little shits! There are no foreign agents, no organization, just a few students recruited from other universities, stupid enough to — how in hell did they do it?

MOHR. *(Faintly amused.)* Now Mahler, are we going to run amok here every time a college student and his professor decide to be unhappy with the government?

MAHLER. An attack on the present government endangers the national security of the country.

MOHR. These kids are just stupid. If we have people prosecuted for stupidity, we'd have to do away with half the world!

MAHLER. That is not an inconceivable thought.

MOHR. I am not a public censor! That's not my job. I only deal with criminals. This is really outside my jurisdiction!

MAHLER. *(Faintly menacing, for the first time.)* Criminal law is not a fixed thing, Herr Mohr. It redefines itself with every age. You are bound by oath to enforce it, or ... I would be glad to accept your resignation and turn it into the Reich Minister of Justice. *(Pause.)*

MOHR. Is that why you are here?

MAHLER. I am here to offer you an option. *(They look at each other. The power has imperceptibly shifted.)* Herr Mohr, why do you find this so difficult? *(Pause.)*

MOHR. Do we have a confession from Professor Huber?

MAHLER. Oh, yes, sir. We have his wife and sister, too, although I don't think they're involved.

MOHR. Why not round up his twelve-year-old daughter, while we're at it? We don't want her getting in contact with Churchill and precipitating the downfall of the Third Reich.

MAHLER. Sir?

MOHR. A joke, Mahler, a joke. Don't you people have a sense of humor?

MAHLER. Humor, sir? At a time like this?

MOHR. What's so different about this time that other times have not seen? Thank you, Mahler, that's all. Oh, by the way ... *(Casually.)* I don't think I'll let you have the girl.

MAHLER. Beg pardon?

MOHR. The girl. You can't have her. We might need her. There will have to be an official statement sooner or later. She'll be very useful.

MAHLER. *(Beat.)* Yes sir. *(An apparent afterthought.)* These people, the Scholls, Graf, Huber, they seem convinced that it's only a matter of weeks before the Allies march on Berlin. I wondered, sir, what is your opinion on that? *(A tense moment.)*

MOHR. I am not a military man. I've no opinions on the matter. I am confident that the Wehrmacht will take care of military strategy appropriately, while we, at home, worry about internal problems the handling of which is what we're paid for.

MAHLER. Of course, sir. *(As Mahler turns to go, Mohr stops him.)*

MOHR. And Mahler ...

MAHLER. Yes, sir?

MOHR. Never ask me a leading question like that again, or I'll have you arrested for insubordination. I haven't tendered my resignation yet.

MAHLER. No, sir. You haven't.

MOHR. That will be all. *(Mahler exits. Mohr paces for a few seconds, then impulsively picks up the phone and dials feverishly. He is perspiring profusely.)* Herta? Talk to me a little.... No, no, just tired. We're all tired. Have you seen Maria today?... Good, good. Yes, it is late, isn't it? The baby — oh, a new tooth! That's wonderful.... Yes, I'll be home tonight. Just a meeting.... Tomorrow? Ah, "Parsifal!" Good, a fairy tale.... Of course it's a fairy tale, don't be silly.... No, a headache.... I'm all right! By the way, have you found my watch yet?... What? No, I — No, no. I'll be on time. The garden gate. Yes, I'll have to fix it. It isn't safe. *(He hangs up the phone. Mumbling.)* ... You put things away for safety, you never find them again ... *(He picks up the paper Mahler had replaced on his desk and reads.)* "Freedom and honor ..." Christ! *(He crumples the paper and hurls it into the wastebasket. There is a knock on the door and Bauer enters.)* Yes?

BAUER.   *(Tonelessly.)* There's a man outside, sir. A Karl Meyer. Press. Wants to see you. About the ... suspects. He's unsure about the press blackout. He was told that publicity of any kind might jam — uh — *delay* — proceedings but he doesn't know where the order came from. Whether it's just local or.... It's unclear, so I told him to talk to you, sir. You're the one. You're the chief. *(Silence.)* What should I say, sir? *(Silence.)* Should I tell him to leave, sir?... Or should he stay? *(Pause.)*

MOHR.   *(Slowly.)* How much does he know?

BAUER.   *(Still without inflection.)* With your permission, sir ... perhaps Herr Mahler has been ... careless. Search parties in students quarters in the middle of the day, sir! That's not how we do things here in Munich. At least, that's the way it looks to me. And it would, to ... other people. After all, sir, you haven't talked to anybody. You haven't even moved from this office. I'm your driver. I'd know. *(Mohr looks closely at Bauer whose face is a blank.)*

MOHR.   Put him in one of the private rooms, on the other side. *(Pause.)* Where is she?

BAUER.   Next door.

MOHR.   Bring her in. *(Bauer exits. The opening chords to the Prelude to* Parsifal *are heard as Bauer returns with Sophie. The church bells outside toll.)* Have you read the statement?

SOPHIE.   Yes. *(He hands her a pen and points to the bottom of the page.)* This last paragraph. It says here that had I understood what the White Rose leaflets were really saying I wouldn't have contributed to —

MOHR.   Yes, that's what it says.

SOPHIE.   *(Beat.)* Has my brother signed?

MOHR. Your brother?

SOPHIE. Yes, has he signed it?

MOHR. Sophie — your brother — ah ... won't be —

SOPHIE. Won't be what?

MOHR. He's hopelessly incriminated. There's nothing I — *(Sophie drops the paper. Outside, the sun shines brighter.)*

SOPHIE. It looks like you're going to have an early spring this year.

MOHR. Yes, no, wait. Please. Listen to me. I can't — *(Takes his voice down.)* All of you — I can't. *Please.* Just listen to — *(He gets on his knees to pick up the statement she'd dropped.)* Will you just — will you sign this?

SOPHIE. Herr Mohr.... If my brother dies, I'll have to die with him.

MOHR. Why!

SOPHIE. That seems to be your favorite question. *(Beat.)* So he wouldn't feel so alone.

MOHR. No, no. Wait. You see ... *(Exploding.)* You can't have it *all!* It can't all be your way! Life just isn't like that! You want everything!

SOPHIE. Yes.

MOHR. You can't — Just sign this thing. Tell them you didn't know what you were doing. You'll go to prison for a while, and —

SOPHIE. But that's not true.

MOHR. I'm sure that if you think about it, you'll see that it's true.

SOPHIE. No.

MOHR. Look —

SOPHIE. No!

MOHR. Why quarrel with a few words that might save your life?

SOPHIE. My word is all I have.

MOHR. Is this all about ... pride?

SOPHIE. *(Pause.)* I — ... a little of that, too.

MOHR. At a time like this?

SOPHIE. It only counts at a time like this. *(Mohr takes the receiver of the telephone off the hook and puts it into his desk drawer.*

He crosses to her.)

MOHR.   *(Very carefully.)* It's possible — there is a chance that
— that Germany might lose the war. All anybody would have
to do who doesn't like the — the present state of things, is
keep his mouth shut, wait it out. *Everything* passes ... in time
... *(Silence.)* The Reich Ministers of Justice and Propaganda do
not like to exercise extreme measures against young Aryan
dissidents who can show that they have been misled by —

SOPHIE.   No, we got them there, didn't we?

MOHR.   Sometimes you sound like your friend Schmorell.
(She reacts. She'd forgotten.)

SOPHIE.   I'd like that. *(Mohr paces. Sophie sits in her chair,
looking at the ground. Pause.)*

MOHR.   Why can't you pretend to go along? Fool everybody.
Have the last laugh.

SOPHIE.   That would mean I was scared of the beast.

MOHR.   Millions of people pretend to go along every day of
their lives so they can survive. Do you think them all beasts?

SOPHIE.   Oh, there are very few "beasts." The real damage
is done by those millions who want to "survive." Those honest men who just want to be left in peace; who don't want
their little lives disturbed by anything bigger than themselves.
Those with no sides, and no causes. Those who won't take the
measure of their own strength for fear of antagonizing their
own shadows. Those who don't like to make waves or enemies. Those for whom passion, truth, freedom, honor, prin-
ciples, are only *literature.* Those for whom everything is "rela-
tive," the excuse of the man with no values. Those who have
no absolutes because their souls can't encompass them. Those
who live small, mate small and die small. The reductionist
approach to life. If you keep it small, you'll keep it under
control. If you don't make any noise, the bogeyman won't
find you. And it's an illusion, because they die too, those
people who rolled up their spirits into tiny little balls to hide
them under their puny lives to be safe. *Safe?*! From what? Life
is always on the edge of death. Narrow streets lead to the
same place as the big, wide avenues, and the little candles
burn themselves out just like the flaming torch. I choose my

own way to burn.

MOHR.   What about the rest of us? Who can't think about "burning up?" Who have a very hard time just — going day to day. Surviving!

SOPHIE.   I don't want to survive, I want to live.

MOHR.   Then sign that goddamn paper and tell them you didn't know what you were doing. You've lied to me for days, you can certainly lie to them.

SOPHIE.   How do you remember who you are, Mohr? How do you keep track of your own soul?

MOHR.   The human race just happens to look like this at the moment. Join the human race, Sophie.

SOPHIE.   Ah, yes! That one! Do something despicable, after all, "it's human!" I don't want to join you!

MOHR.   I have always tried my best to —

SOPHIE.   You haven't tried your best! Your best is with your *life* and you haven't tried with your life!

MOHR.   I'm like everybody else out there! I'm not God! I'm a civil servant! A simple man with a job. And I can't give it up whenever — because — things — change. I — I don't — I don't join movements, and I don't sign petitions! I don't put my name to — my *wife* signs my Christmas cards! I would do anything — *anything* to survive! You say I look the other way? Not really. Most of us are not given clarity of vision in the midst of chaos. That is only possible in extreme youth or in extreme belief. Extreme youth lasts a moment —

SOPHIE.   Then I only want to last that perfect moment!

MOHR.   — and extreme belief is something most people cannot sustain. Like "perfection," it wears off with the years.

SOPHIE.   It's let go of. Like falling asleep in the snow.

MOHR.   If you don't let go of it it'll kill you. You look the Gorgon in the face and you die, Sophie. And nothing is worth your life. *Nothing!* What makes death a victory?

SOPHIE.   Civilization!

MOHR.   I am not "civilization" goddamnit! I am not a dis-embodied concept! I am a man! I want to live! I have a family, I want *them* to live! Grow up! What do you think you're accomplishing? What's it all for?

SOPHIE. To remind people.

MOHR. Of what?

SOPHIE. That we make the world, not the other way around.

MOHR. *(Exploding.)* To what avail, Sophie, to what avail?

SOPHIE. It's the right thing to do! It's ... right!

MOHR. How in hell do you come to know what's "right" so absolutely?

SOPHIE. I don't know! It's an instinct! I don't know!

MOHR. Life is a *median* thing, Sophie. Those who need to live it banners flying high in the wind, always end up being tripped by the others ... those who have no room for passion of *any* kind: the majority, who have their feet planted firm on the ground and their eyes steadily half-way up. Don't make me trip you, Sophie. I'm trying to save your life. *(Pause.)*

SOPHIE. *(Quietly.)* You wouldn't save my brother, you wouldn't save a Jew. You can't save me.

MOHR. You're not a Jew!

SOPHIE. Yes, I am. Today I am my brother and I am a Jew. You're not trying to save me, you're trying to save yourself.

MOHR. From what?!

SOPHIE. You tell me.

MOHR. ... Bauer! Bauer! *(Bauer enters alarmed.)* GET THIS BITCH OUT OF HERE! *(Bauer takes Sophie out. Mahler appears at the door. Mohr gathers the papers on his desk and begins to sign them.)* Here are the indictments. Take them.

MAHLER. Any amendments, sir?

MOHR. None.

MAHLER. Extenuating circumstances?

MOHR. None. TAKE THEM! *(Mohr shoves the papers in Mahler's direction who takes them and exits. Bauer re-enters.)*

BAUER. Excuse me, sir. That press man. Outside. He's waiting. *(Mohr looks at him a moment. Then shakes his head "no.")* Sir?

MOHR. *(Almost inaudibly.)* No. *(Pause.)*

BAUER. *(Unsteady.)* Of course, sir. I just thought I'd check with you, sir. I don't do anything without checking. *(A beat.*

Bauer hesitates, then exits. Mohr puts his head in his hands. Black-
out. The bells from the Frauenkirche are heard.)

DAY 5 — MONDAY, FEBRUARY 22, 1943

Lights on Sophie in her cell.

SOPHIE. I love early mornings. I love dancing with a man
cheek to cheek. Men's faces ... just shaved, a little rough. The
scent of tobacco and cologne. I wonder what it would have
been like having a child, or stalking the tiger in Burma; crossing the high seas in a twenty-foot clipper, hearing the "Missa
Solemnis" in St. Stephen's Cathedral, or the bells of Notre
Dame at midnight on Christmas Eve. I love the fur on the
head of my dog Freddie. He always smells "doggie." I love
that. And the smell of fresh coffee, too. And jasmine. Oh, I
wish I could remember everything I've loved, but there isn't
enough time. There is never enough time. Now I understand
the deep stab of pain I have felt whenever I've looked on
great beauty. We take leave of everything we love, just as we
embrace it for the first time. *(Pause.)* I have never loved life
so much. *(Beat.)* Oh, God, my parents ... *(She hides her face in
her hands. Lights up on Mohr and Bauer. While Mohr talks Bauer
stands at attention, stone-faced.)*
MOHR. *(Detached.)* She stood up to Freisler. Imagine! That
slip of a girl, standing up to Freisler in a trial for her life.
Jumped to her feet and said right to his face: "Well, somebody had to make a start!" Right to his face. And Bauer, you
should have seen him, shrieking about treason and sabotage,
all red in the face. But he never looked her in the eye....
They were so alone, sitting there in the midst — *but not adrift*
— a sea of uniforms, brown, grey, black. And that screaming
judge. And suddenly this terrible voice was heard from the
back of the courtroom. It was the father. "Tell that man I am
here to defend my children!" A lion looking for its cubs. He
looked like ... a god. I've never seen a man look like that....
When they dragged him out he was shouting "They will go

down in history!" They were taken out manacled, and Scholl grabbed the hands of his brother who had pushed his way through the crowd and said "Don't give in!" In handcuffs, condemned to death ... still fighting! I think I   understand — I mean, look at that father. I've a daughter who ... *(Silence. Bauer clears his throat and keeps looking straight ahead. Mahler enters with new files. Pause.)* Will they hang them?

MAHLER.   No, they will be guillotined.

MOHR.   They're Germans, Mahler! Surely they can be put away somewhere ... forgotten?

MAHLER.   Forgotten?... They haven't happened. *(Pause.)*

MOHR.   Has the time been set?

MAHLER.   This afternoon. Five o'clock.

MOHR.   Doesn't that strike you as a bit ... frantic?

MAHLER.   No, sir. Efficient.

MOHR.   *(Abruptly.)* What shall we do?

MAHLER.   Sir?

MOHR.   What?

MAHLER.   "Do?"

MOHR.   No.... Where are they?

MAHLER.   Stadelheim Prison, sir, for execution.

MOHR.   Have their families been alerted?

MAHLER.   We don't want to make any more of this than we need to.

MOHR.   "We?"

MAHLER.   Oh, Berlin, sir. Now I have here another list of names: Wittenstein, Hirzel, Schertling —

MOHR.   What are they doing?

MAHLER.   Pardon?

MOHR.   Those kids. What are they doing?

MAHLER.   I don't — they seem uncommonly calm, sir.

MOHR.   Yes ... from the beginning. I should have known. A pride of lions. Graceful. Graceful! What, with the price of grace these days ... *(He quickly goes for his aspirin bottle in his desk drawer but it's empty. He pours a glass of water and drinks it. He seems out of breath.)*

MAHLER.   Sir, are you —

MOHR.   Perfectly fine! What else today?

MAHLER. This new list of suspects —

MOHR. What's the date?

MAHLER. *(Puzzled.)* February 22, sir.

MOHR. Five days.

MAHLER. What?

MOHR. I've known them only five days. *(Looking out the window.)* Still winter. Beautiful day. So bright. Such deep colors. *(He listens.)* A bird. On that tree. *(Disoriented.)* This office needs painting. Everything is so *clear* today!... Except this picture of me. *(He picks it up.)* Third from the left. Graduation. Police Academy. I was twenty-one. It's blurred. I think I need glasses. Time. Decay. Everything passes, Mahler. *(An edge.)* Remember that.

MAHLER. Why don't I come back later ...

MOHR. *(Suddenly.)* I've got to go to Stadelheim.

MAHLER. What for? You're fin —

MOHR. I've got to get to Stadelheim. *(But he sits behind his desk, and begins to drink his coffee. Mahler watches him.)*

MAHLER. They ... believed in something ... and I believe in something else. What has been puzzling me these last few days, is that I haven't the slightest idea of what in hell you believe in, Mohr. *(Outside, the Church of Our Lady begins to toll its bells for five o'clock. U.C. an individual spotlight comes up on Hans.)*

HANS. *(Both arms up.)* Long live freedom! *(His spotlight goes out with the first bell toll. Mohr grabs the sides of his desk tight with both hands, as if to steady himself.)*

MOHR. Believe? Now, *that's* odd ... vocabulary. For the times. *(Distracted.)* I'm a simple man. *(On another part of the stage a single spotlight on Probst.)*

PROBST. *(Gently.)* It's easier than I thought. *(His spotlight goes out. Second bell toll. Mohr reacts every time. Mahler does not.)*

MOHR. I'm a simple man. If there ever was anything bigger than my simple life, I never saw it. It never spoke to me. I never heard it.

MAHLER. You seemed to take a particular interest in the girl, sir.

MOHR. I have a daughter her age. She's a rather bovine

creature who waddles through life glassy-eyed and un-rousable, like most of us. She'll live long and wrinkle late. *(A single spot-light on Willi Graf.)*

WILLI.   God have mercy on my soul. *(He crosses himself. Third bell toll.)*

MOHR.   Have you ever been face to face with ... *passion?*

MAHLER.   *(Puzzled.)* Passion? If you would sign this, sir.

MOHR.   *(Absently.)* I never sign anything — what is it?

MAHLER.   A formality, sir. A bill, to the families. For the use and clean up of the instrument.

MOHR.   The what?

MAHLER.   The blade, sir ... *(Pause. Mohr stares at Mahler.)* Sir?... Sir!

MOHR.   Yes. *(He signs without looking, and pushes the paper away.)*

MAHLER.   About this list, sir. *(He pulls it out of his pocket.)* There is no copy of it just yet. It's been scribbled by one of my agents as he took the names down. There are some eighty suspects, so —

MOHR.   Leave it on my desk. Close the office, Bauer, I'm going home early. *(Bauer exits.)* And Mahler, to answer your earlier question: I believe what most of us believe. I believe in trying my best — no, in getting by. Yes. The most we can hope for is to get by. Heroes and ... *(Carefully.)* demagogues will always shake things up for a while, but if we're clever, we'll still be here when they're gone. After all, there's more of us than there are of them. Long after they've ... "burned up" ... we'll still be around, just getting by. *(A spotlight on Schmorell.)*

SCHMORELL.   Friedrich Schiller, Ludwig Van Beethoven, Heinrich Heine ... *(His spotlight goes out. Fourth bell toll.)*

MAHLER.   *(Very pleasantly.)* You mustn't underestimate yourself, sir. People like you are of enormous use to the Reich. Why ... we wouldn't be here without you. *(Mahler smiles, and puts the list on the desk. He salutes and Mohr turns away from him to look out the window. Mahler exits. Mohr gets his coat, hat and gloves. Bauer enters.)*

MOHR.   I have to fix my garden gate.

BAUER. Yes, sir. (*Bauer exits and returns with a large trash bag, as Mohr starts putting on his coat.*)

MOHR. What did you think of them, Bauer?

BAUER. (*Going about his business of cleaning up.*) Who, sir?

MOHR. The ... those kids. What did you think of them?

BAUER. (*Continuing to clean.*) Think, sir? Oh, I don't know. Cocky little bastards.

MOHR. (*Absent-mindedly.*) Yes. (*Looking around.*) Well ... nothing's changed then. Everything stays the same.

BAUER. Oh, no, sir. The janitor got a medal.

MOHR. Who?

BAUER. Schmidt. 3,000 marks ...

MOHR. (*Beat.*) Yes ... (*He looks out the window.*) It's gone.

BAUER. Sir?

MOHR. So quiet. What time is it? I don't have a watch.

BAUER. (*With difficulty.*) Five o'clock, sir.

MOHR. (*Putting on his hat and coat.*) Good afternoon, Bauer. (*A spotlight on Sophie.*)

SOPHIE. This is *my* time.... This is the best of me. (*Her spotlight goes out with the fifth bell toll.*)

MOHR. (*Walking out.*) I wonder what's for dinner. (*Mohr exits. Bauer stands still for a moment, and the vacant look leaves his face. He quickly goes through the papers on the desk. He picks up the list that Mahler had left. He reads it and using his cigarette lighter, sets fire to it, and drops it in the wastepaper basket. He exits dragging the trash bag and whistling the Beethoven Ninth. Behind him, the paper burns in the basket. U.C. the shadow of the crossed out swastika they had painted on the wall is the last visible thing on stage.*)

END OF PLAY

PROPERTY LIST

White leaflets
Small suitcase (SOPHIE)
Identification photos
Pile of report folders
Large dictionary (BAUER)
Report folder with papers
Phonograph and records
Bottle of wine (HANS)
Corkscrew (HANS)
Baby photos (PROBST)
Glasses for wine
Old mimeograph machine (SCHMORELL)
Bottle of aspirins (MOHR)
Decanter of wine (MOHR)
Glasses for water (MOHR)
Book (SOPHIE)
Cigarettes (MAHLER)
Lighter or matches (MAHLER)
Binoculars (SCHMORELL)
Flashlight
Small wild flower (SCHMORELL)
Small black notebook (MAHLER)
Pen (MAHLER)
Papers (MAHLER)
Coffee in mug (MOHR)
Large trash bag (BAUER)
Overcoat, hat and gloves (MOHR)
Cigarette lighter (BAUER)

SOUND EFFECTS

Church bells: striking the hour and half-hour
Alarm bells
Doors closing
Gates clanking shut
Phone ring
Crowd shouts: "Sieg Heil!'"
Muffled voice of Adolf Hitler with crowd
War planes flying past
Cell doors clanging shut
Air-raid siren
Bomb blasts
Police sirens (distant and close)
Gun fire
Marching boots
Trucks passing
Footsteps
Bird singing

NEW PLAYS

★ **INTIMATE APPAREL by Lynn Nottage.** The moving and lyrical story of a turn-of-the-century black seamstress whose gifted hands and sewing machine are the tools she uses to fashion her dreams from the whole cloth of her life's experiences. "…Nottage's play has a delicacy and eloquence that seem absolutely right for the time she is depicting…" *–NY Daily News.* "…thoughtful, affecting…The play offers poignant commentary on an era when the cut and color of one's dress—and of course, skin—determined whom one could and could not marry, sleep with, even talk to in public." *–Variety.* [2M, 4W] ISBN: 0-8222-2009-1

★ **BROOKLYN BOY by Donald Margulies.** A witty and insightful look at what happens to a writer when his novel hits the bestseller list. "The characters are beautifully drawn, the dialogue sparkles…" *–nytheatre.com.* "Few playwrights have the mastery to smartly investigate so much through a laugh-out-loud comedy that combines the vintage subject matter of successful writer-returning-to-ethnic-roots with the familiar mid-life crisis." *–Show Business Weekly.* [4M, 3W] ISBN: 0-8222-2074-1

★ **CROWNS by Regina Taylor.** Hats become a springboard for an exploration of black history and identity in this celebratory musical play. "Taylor pulls off a Hat Trick: She scores thrice, turning CROWNS into an artful amalgamation of oral history, fashion show, and musical theater…" *–TheatreMania.com.* "…wholly theatrical…Ms. Taylor has created a show that seems to arise out of spontaneous combustion, as if a bevy of department-store customers simultaneously decided to stage a revival meeting in the changing room." *–NY Times.* [1M, 6W (2 musicians)] ISBN: 0-8222-1963-8

★ **EXITS AND ENTRANCES by Athol Fugard.** The story of a relationship between a young playwright on the threshold of his career and an aging actor who has reached the end of his. "[Fugard] can say more with a single line than most playwrights convey in an entire script…Paraphrasing the title, it's safe to say this drama, making its memorable entrance into our consciousness, is unlikely to exit as long as a theater exists for exceptional work." *–Variety.* "A thought-provoking, elegant and engrossing new play…" *–Hollywood Reporter.* [2M] ISBN: 0-8222-2041-5

★ **BUG by Tracy Letts.** A thriller featuring a pair of star-crossed lovers in an Oklahoma City motel facing a bug invasion, paranoia, conspiracy theories and twisted psychological motives. "…obscenely exciting…top-flight craftsmanship. Buckle up and brace yourself…" *–NY Times.* "…[a] thoroughly outrageous and thoroughly entertaining play…the possibility of enemies, real and imagined, to squash has never been more theatrical." *–A.P.* [3M, 2W] ISBN: 0-8222-2016-4

★ **THOM PAIN (BASED ON NOTHING) by Will Eno.** An ordinary man muses on childhood, yearning, disappointment and loss, as he draws the audience into his last-ditch plea for empathy and enlightenment. "It's one of those treasured nights in the theater—treasured nights anywhere, for that matter—that can leave you both breathless with exhilaration and…in a puddle of tears." *–NY Times.* "Eno's words…are familiar, but proffered in a way that is constantly contradictory to our expectations. Beckett is certainly among his literary ancestors." *–nytheatre.com.* [1M] ISBN: 0-8222-2076-8

★ **THE LONG CHRISTMAS RIDE HOME by Paula Vogel.** Past, present and future collide on a snowy Christmas Eve for a troubled family of five. "…[a] lovely and hauntingly original family drama…a work that breathes so much life into the theater." *–Time Out.* "…[a] delicate visual feast…" *–NY Times.* "…brutal and lovely…the overall effect is magical." *–NY Newsday.* [3M, 3W] ISBN: 0-8222-2003-2

DRAMATISTS PLAY SERVICE, INC.
440 Park Avenue South, New York, NY 10016 212-683-8960 Fax 212-213-1539
postmaster@dramatists.com www.dramatists.com